RESTORED

A LIFE BETTER THAN BEFORE

DR. ROBERT GAY

Melbourne, Florida
Published and Printed in the USA.

Restored—A Life Better Than Before
by Robert Gay

Parsons Publishing House
P. O. Box 410063
Melbourne, FL 32940 USA
Info@ParsonsPublishingHouse.com

Publisher has opted to reference satan and related names with lowercase letters.

Cover Art by Micah Gay.

ISBN-13: 978-160273-178-3
ISBN-10: 160273178-0
Library of Congress Control Number: 2025944053
Printed in the United States of America.
For World-Wide Distribution.

TABLE OF CONTENTS

RESTORED

INTRODUCTION

> "'For I will restore health to you and heal you of your wounds,' says the LORD, 'Because they called you an outcast saying: "This is Zion; No one seeks her."'" "Thus says the LORD: 'Behold, I will bring back the captivity of Jacob's tents, And have mercy on his dwelling places;'"(Jeremiah 30:17-18a).

Have you ever known anyone whose life has fallen apart? Perhaps you were that person, or it was a friend or family member. The truth is we have either known someone or been the person whose life was in shambles and needed help. It is plain to see that we live in a world full of broken people who need to be restored and made whole.

We witness this on a regular basis wherever we go. It is not just individuals, but also families, workplaces, media, government, and other various systems of man that are fractured and need repairing. There are hurt people everywhere doing things that are painful to others. Things are said and done daily that result in damage to people's personage and property. Just one hour of any news broadcast will confirm this to be true.

It requires little discernment to realize we live in a crazy world. Scrolling through our social media feed reveals that we live in a world that needs restoring. Our neighborhoods and schools are filled with people who need God to repair the broken places within their lives.

When Adam and Eve sinned in the garden, the entire Earth was sent into a cataclysmic shift, which resulted in pain and heartache for everyone. God declared that because of Adam's sin, there would be thorns and thistles, the things that bring pain. Adam and Eve were removed from their God-given paradise, the Garden of Eden, and placed into a world that would be ruled by the curse. It was all the consequence of their own disobedience.

Jesus Came to Restore

The good news is that in the fullness of time, Jesus came to redeem mankind from that curse. He came to restore what man lost in the fall. He came to put the broken things back together. Jesus was sent to repair the breach between God and man; He came to right what was wrong. Jesus came to restore!

Sin produced significant damage within the earth and still does today. Every evil that mankind experiences can be traced back to the original sin of Adam. We are brought into a fallen world that is filled with wickedness. Jesus came to rescue man from the curse that sin brought and place him back into a right relationship with God. He did what was needed to accomplish this through His death, burial, and victorious resurrection.

It is imperative we understand that Jesus is the Restorer, not the destroyer. He came to restore man back to the place from where he fell. This is an attribute of God's character that needs to be declared and emphasized today. Jesus came to restore everything that the devil stole. Jesus said that He came to seek and to save that which was lost. He desires for you to walk in the abundant life that was purchased at Calvary.

Biblical Principles to Enact Restoration

There are biblical principles which can be enacted that will empower and release God's restorative grace to accomplish its work. These are truths that will bring freedom, healing, and deliverance within the lives of believers. Jesus said that you will know the truth, and the truth will set you free. It is the knowledge and application of biblical truths that will change your life and enable you to be restored.

There are seven primary principles that we are going to discuss throughout this book, which will empower this restoration in your life. Here are the principles listed in order:

1. Forgive those who have wronged you.
2. Refuse to live as a victim.
3. Confront generational and family issues.
4. Receive biblical identity by renewing the mind.
5. Speak the right words—God's Word.
6. Receive emotional healing.
7. Embrace deliverance and freedom.

These principles embody biblical truths that will heal and liberate those who are bound. Restoration will be realized, and a new way of living will begin as these things are put into practice.

Jesus Makes Things Better

God intends to make your life better than it was before. He always makes things greater once He touches them. Jesus turned five loaves and two fish into something much larger. He fed over five thousand people with what was small and insignificant. He desires to make your life better. Yes, Jesus wants to restore you!

My wife, Stacey, and I have personally experienced this within our lives. We have also seen thousands of others receive healing, deliverance, and restoration as they embraced these truths. They experienced restoration in their marriages, families, businesses, health, and finances as they implemented these proven principles of Christianity.

God's will for your life is restoration. He wants to heal you of every hurt that you have within every part of your being. This is part of your redemption that was purchased through the blood of Jesus. You can say "so long and goodbye" to the pain of yesterday and fully embrace the future that God has prepared for you. It can start right now!

Make a determination of heart to apply God's Word in your life. Refuse merely to be a hearer of the Word; choose to be a doer of it, too! The person who only hears will end up with a house in shambles. However, the person who practices the principles that Jesus taught and demonstrated will be blessed and restored. The choice is yours. What do you desire?

Today, you can begin a journey to see everything restored in your life. Regardless of what may have happened in your past, God desires to make it better than it has ever been before. He wants you to receive the fullness of everything that He paid for through His redemptive work.

Position your heart to receive and practice all the things set out in this book, and you will see God do a mighty work in your life. This is the day, now is the time, and this is the moment that God has ordained for you to receive restoration. Seize this opportunity and let God do a mighty work within your life. This is your moment to be RESTORED!

RESTORED

1

Better Than Before

> "So I will restore to you the years that the swarming locust has eaten, The crawling locust, The consuming locust, And the chewing locust, My great army which I sent among you. You shall eat in plenty and be satisfied, And praise the name of the LORD your God, Who has dealt wondrously with you; And My people shall never be put to shame. Then you shall know that I am in the midst of Israel: I am the LORD your God And there is no other. My people shall never be put to shame" (Joel 2:25-27).

Throughout history, God revealed Himself as the God of Restoration. We can observe this truth in operation within the lives of biblical patriarchs such as Noah, Abraham, Job, and Joseph, to name a few. He desires to restore His people. This is an underlying attribute of His character and nature. It is a dimension that we, as Christians, should embrace and cherish as part of the unchangeable nature of God.

There are many in the body of Christ who fail to see the Lord in this manner. Their perception of God is one of an angry old man sitting on His front porch, daring anyone to set foot in his yard. Anyone who trespasses will cause wrath and indignation to rain down like no one has ever seen before. This is an unfortunate image that so many have of the Lord today.

God's character is diametrically opposed to the proverbial angry old man sitting on the porch with a shotgun. He actually has a sign in the yard that says, *"All are welcome!"* He is not looking for an opportunity to punish, judge, or inflict pain on anyone. His nature is the exact opposite of this.

God desires to bless, forgive, and heal. His will is to repair what has been damaged and fix the brokenness. He is not a God who kicks people when they are down; rather, He lifts them up and binds their wounds. Our God is a Restorer!

The Names of God Reveal His Nature

Most Christians are familiar with what we have termed as the redemptive names of God. *Jehovah-Jireh* is the Lord who sees and provides. *Jehovah-Shamma* is the Lord who is present with us. *Jehovah-Rapha* is the Lord who heals our bodies. There are more redemptive and descriptive names that we could mention, but these are some of the names that are more commonly understood and used among believers today. I have personally written songs that embody these redemptive names.

All the names of God mentioned in the Bible are there for one primary purpose: to reveal the nature and character of God. They show us who God desires to be within our lives and what He is willing and ready to do. They cause our faith to be built, strengthened, and stirred to receive the fullness of His working in our lives and families. Every redemptive name is intended to give us the ability to put our faith in the NAME of the Lord, to depend on Him to be all that we need.

Believe in the Name of the Lord

We are repeatedly admonished in God's Word to trust and believe in the name of the Lord. That means we are to put our trust in the fullness of His character revealed through His redemptive names. We do not only believe that He saved us from sin (*Jehovah-Tsidkenu*), but we also believe that He saves us from sickness (*Jehovah-Rapha*) and poverty (*Jehovah-Jireh*). We put our trust in His name by believing He will do what His names reveal.

So, believing in the name of the Lord means that we learn, study, meditate, and receive the Lord in the fullness of His nature, as is revealed through His names. We trust in the fullness of His nature. We rest in not only the promise He made, but also His character displayed and revealed through His names. Our faith moves beyond just His spoken word to equally rest in the person we know as Jesus Christ, the very Son of God.

As I said previously, there are several names of God that are well-known by Christians. *Jehovah Shalom*, the Lord our peace, is a familiar name that many believers refer to when they are going through stressful and anxiety-filled situations. We rehearse that name because it brings the surety of His peace into our hearts. It brings an awareness of His peace, which passes all understanding, that is designed to rule our hearts and minds. We trust Him to be our peace and bring resolution to our circumstances. However, there are many that are not as familiar.

Jehovah-*SHALAM*

There is a name of which most believers are not familiar. That name encompasses God's power and ability to restore—to put things back together better than they were previously. That name is *Jehovah-SHALAM*, the God who restores. It is interwoven and connected with the name *Jehovah-Shalom*. The reason for this is that *SHALAM* is the Hebrew root word for *shalom*. *Shalom* is derived from *SHALAM*. At the root of God's peace is His power and ability to restore. Although *Jehovah-SHALAM* is not specifically found in a verse of Scripture, it is no less biblical in its truth.

He is not just *Jehovah-Shalom*, the God, our peace; He is also *Jehovah-SHALAM*, the God who restores. He desires to restore anything and everything that is broken. Jesus wants to put things back together in your life, family, finances, marriage, and health. His delight is to restore things in a manner that is better than what they were previously. Anything that has been stolen from you, God desires for it to be returned to you with interest!

The reason I know this is simply because this is His nature; it is His character. I also know it because I have personally experienced this within my own life and seen it happen in many others. This is the way He functions and operates. Jesus did not come to destroy; He came to restore. He is not the destroyer, but rather the restorer.

You may ask, "*Why is it so important to know this?*" The answer is simply that we cannot receive anything from the Lord until we know that it is His will. Our faith can never move beyond the revealed knowledge of the will of God. Therefore, we must know and be fully persuaded that God will restore us. It must be well rooted in our spirit man that whatever has been stolen from us or done to us, God will bring restoration and make it better than before.

Wrong Perspective

There are many people who view the Lord from a lens where everything that happens in their lives is God's divine plan. Therefore, the pain and grief that they suffered in the past were all a part of God's will for their lives. They believe, in some way or another, that God orchestrated every event they ever experienced, even destruction and pain.

Unfortunately, this perspective causes people to view the Lord as a marionette puppeteer who divinely leads them down painful roads of devastation. They see God as the destroyer rather than the restorer. Their trust in the name of the Lord is hindered because they are convinced that God ordained their hurtful experiences. They separate themselves from any wrong choices they make or just the effects of living in a fallen world. Instead, their finger is pointed at God for being the author of their painful situation. My friend, this line of thinking is not the truth.

Our God is a good Father, not an abusive dad. Jesus repeatedly said that He would bless us, not orchestrate bad things to teach us something and beat us into submission. He continued by saying that the Heavenly Father would give us good things if we asked Him, not painful things. God is good, and His mercy endures forever. His goodness did not run out when you showed up; it is still present and always near you.

Restore Defined

There are two different Hebrew words that are translated as "restore." The first word is *shub*, which means to turn back (like you would turn back a clock). It is best described as a reset. You go back to square one before things were lost or stolen.

The other Hebrew word translated as "restore" is *SHALAM*, which I mentioned previously. When it is translated as "restore" in the Old Testament, it primarily refers to receiving more than what one had previously. In other words, you get back what was stolen with interest. The latter state of the person or situation is better and more glorious than before. Simply put, more than you had before!

Let me give you some biblical examples of where the word *SHALAM* is translated as "restore." You will see in these instances that the meaning of the word is to have more and greater.

> "If a man steals an ox or a sheep, and slaughters it or sells it, he shall restore [*SHALAM*] five oxen..." (Exodus 22:1, emphasis added).

> "If the theft is certainly found...whether it is an ox or donkey or sheep, he shall restore [*SHALAM*] double" (Exodus 22:4, emphasis added)

> "... all that about which he has sworn falsely. He shall restore [*SHALAM*] its full value, add one-fifth more to it..." (Leviticus 6:5, emphasis added).
>
> "Yet when he is found, he must restore [*SHALAM*] sevenfold; He may have to give up all the substance of his house" (Proverbs 6:31, emphasis added).

In all of these verses of Scripture, the word "restore" is the Hebrew word *SHALAM*. You can easily see how God commanded that when there was a loss through thievery, there was to be recompense executed with interest. The victims were to be given more than they had before—greater than they possessed previously.

We not only see this written as part of Levitical Law, but also as a principle that Solomon wrote of in the book of Proverbs. He articulated something more than merely the given law and precept; he communicated it as a spiritual principle at work. The thief must restore sevenfold. That means seven times better and greater than the previous. Hallelujah.

The Devil Is a Thief

As believers today, we understand that satan and his demons are thieves. They come to rob, steal, kill, and destroy. They have no good intentions and only seek to harm. The devil desires to produce chaos and havoc in the lives of Christians and anyone else that he can. Unfortunately, some believers become victimized by the strategies of the enemy because they are not fully fortified and do not know how to ward off demonic attacks. However, as believers, this should not be the story of our lives.

As those who are washed in the blood of Jesus and in covenant with God, we have a redemptive right to stand and command restoration, the *SHALAM* of heaven. We can put our faith and trust in *Jehovah-SHALAM*—the God who restores—and experience God's power in every area of our lives. Regardless of what has happened and whose fault it may be, God will restore more than you had before!

I believe that Christians can expect God to do this within their lives. If God commanded that there be a "*SHALAM*" in the Old Testament, how much more will He do it now? We have a better covenant that is established upon better promises. Think about it!

Hurricane Michael

On October 10, 2018, Hurricane Michael, a Category 5 tropical cyclone, hit the Panhandle of Florida. The eye of the storm that packed 165 mph winds and gusts near 200 mph went directly over the eastern part of Bay County, Florida. It just so happened that the eye of the storm passed immediately over my home and the church building where my wife and I pastored. Our entire area was devastated. It looked like an atomic bomb had exploded in our region, and we were ground zero. Most things within a 10–20-mile radius of the eye of the storm sustained catastrophic damage. It was terrifying and heartbreaking.

My wife and our family evacuated during the storm and retreated to Orlando. We watched on television as Hurricane

Michael traveled its path to the Panhandle of Florida. A Category 5 hurricane causes catastrophic damage (only four Category 5 storms have hit the U.S. mainland since 1851). So, we prayed for protection, waited for it to pass, and believed for the best.

I Will Restore to You

When pictures came back of the sheer devastation, the Lord gave me a prophetic word for our congregation and the people of the area. The Lord spoke to me the Scripture found in Joel 2:25, "I will restore to you." I shared the word in a video on Facebook® and encouraged our congregation in Panama City, along with the entire region. I still have very vivid memories of that moment. Here is what I prophesied:

> *Do not be discouraged or disheartened, for you will arise out of the ashes. My glory will arise upon you in a new and greater measure. Do not fear, for I am with you. Surely, you will see a turnaround, and out of destruction will arise a new city, new people, and new season. Poverty will be turned to wealth and darkness to light. Surely you will recover, and for your shame, I will restore double honor.*

At the time I gave this prophetic word, I did not fully know everything that God meant when I spoke it. Often, prophets and prophetic voices can speak without possessing full comprehension of what God is saying. Paul said, "We know in part, and we prophesy in part."

The Revelation of *SHALAM*

It was weeks later that I felt impressed by the Lord to do a word study specifically on the word "restore." The Hebrew word translated "restore" in Joel 2:25 is *SHALAM*. It was only then I discovered that when this word is translated as "restore," it typically means to have a greater amount than you had previously—more than you had before. This was quickened to me, and I started declaring that we would have more than we had before. Our entire church body started using the word "*SHALAM*" and saying that we would have more than we had before.

As time went by, there were testimonies of people who received large settlements and payouts that resulted in their homes ending up in a better condition than they were before the hurricane. The testimonies poured in from people concerning the restoration of their properties. Their situations on the other side of the storm were better than they had been prior to the devastation. Many businesses and private contractors secured more contracts and made more money than they had in the history of their businesses. God fulfilled His Word; He did what He said He would do.

Our church was not only able to repair and restore the damaged things, but we were able to eliminate the remaining debt on our building. We also ended up with more than double the amount of money in our bank account than we had before the storm. My wife and I were able to repair the damage at our home and have funds left over for improvements. God did exactly what He said, and we had more than we had before. Hallelujah!

It is important for believers to understand that God's character and nature are to restore. It is impossible for Him to do anything else. He does not come to destroy. That is not who He is or will ever be.

The Restoration of Job

When we look at the account of Job that we read in the Bible, we see the nature of God revealed. We can witness this principle of restoration exhibited and put on display. Many people read the story of Job and see it as an account of devastation and destruction. However, they fail to read the last chapter. In the end, God restores everything that was stolen in a double portion manner. Job experiences *Jehovah-SHALAM*, the God who restores.

In this biblical story, satan ravages the life and possessions of Job; he loses everything. His wife tells him to curse God and die. She encourages him to point the finger and blame God, but Job refuses to do so and maintains his integrity. He continues to serve God and perseveres in his belief that God will do him good in the end.

Job's life is similar to the reality that all of us live with today. We live in a fallen world where there is demonic activity that attempts to ravage the lives and families of individuals. Things happen sometimes which we may not understand. However, God will restore if we persevere. He already has planned the end from the beginning. His end desire for all of us is to see full restoration and have more and better than we had before.

> Indeed we count them blessed who endure. You have heard of the perseverance of Job and seen the end intended by the Lord—that the Lord is very compassionate and merciful (James 5:11).

This is the only verse of Scripture in the New Testament concerning the life of Job. There is only one thing that is specifically pointed out about him: he persevered. In other words, Job did not quit or stop believing God. His faith was firmly rooted in the belief that God was good and should be glorified.

God Intended to Restore

The other thing many people overlook in the above verse of Scripture is that God had an intended end. God already planned to restore Job's losses before the first thing was ever stolen. Before his day of adversity, God already planned victory. Restoration was the intended end before the entire ordeal started. Hallelujah!

The fact is everyone has experienced loss, pain, and destruction in some way or another. We have all been through hurtful situations that have damaged our personage or possessions, and many times both. However, that does not have to be the end of the story. It is not the conclusion of the book of your life. God has plans to restore you to better than before. *Jehovah-SHALAM* wants to show up and show out!

Job had a chance to get bitter. Instead, he chose to get better. Job had a chance to curse. Instead, he chose to bless. Job had a chance to become angry at his fair-weather friends. Instead, he chose to love them regardless of their displayed ignorance. He maintained the right attitude and disposition in the middle of his trial. He knew that he served the God who restores!

We Have All Experienced Pain

Every human alive on the earth has experienced some sort of pain in their life. It starts from the time you are born into this world. Think about this. When a baby is born, it is a painful experience for both mother and infant. The mother undergoes intense contractions and pushing that are difficult and exhausting. The infant travels through a very tight place, arriving in a cold delivery room only to be scrubbed, poked, and prodded by doctors and nurses.

As we travel the road of life, things happen to us. All these experiences have an effect that shapes our personage. In a fallen world, there are bad people who do terrible things. There are hurt people who, in turn, do hurtful things. There are dishonest people who steal and conniving people who use, abuse, and manipulate others. We encounter these diverse types of people throughout our lives, and it has a profound negative impact on us.

Just like Job, we have a choice. We can bless, forgive, persevere, and then see restoration, or we can curse, become bitter, and end up living with our pain until the day we die. We can embrace *Jehovah-SHALAM* to see restoration, or we can embrace our pain and hurt to see destruction. The choice we make will determine our outcome.

God is placing a choice in front of you today. There is life and death, blessing and cursing, restoration and pain. Which do you desire?

Pray This

"God, I receive you as Jehovah-SHALAM, the God who restores. Come and revolutionize every part of my life. Create within me a clean heart and renew a right spirit within me. I thank You that Your process of restoration starts in me today. I receive it in Jesus' name!"

2

Forgiveness—The Key to Restoration

"If you forgive the sins of any, they are forgiven them; if you retain the sins of any, they are retained" (John 20:23).

Forgiveness is so important in the life of any Christian. When we consider the fact that our salvation is based on God's forgiveness extended to us, we recognize this principle as a foundational cornerstone. Our relationship with Jesus is built upon the fact that He forgave us. Without forgiveness, we stand outside the family of God. Without forgiveness, redemption does not exist.

It is forgiveness extended to us that makes a way for us to be born again and experience the very nature of God. Eternal life is a gift that is given to those who are forgiven. God's mercy and grace manifest through forgiveness extended to all who will repent.

The same forgiveness that we have received is what we should now extend to others. Just as God unconditionally forgives us of our sins, so we must do the same with those who have wronged us. Forgiveness is not predicated on the apology issued to us by another. It is an act of obedience because we have been forgiven.

Jesus Emphasized Forgiveness

Jesus repeatedly emphasized the act of forgiving others. It is more than a suggestion; it is a command that has been given to all. There are over a dozen different biblical references where Jesus instructed people to forgive others and not hold an offense or grudge. He repeatedly declared that it is wrong to seek revenge or even pray for revenge to be taken upon those who have wronged us. Seeking or hoping that those who have sinned against us will receive a payback reveals the absence of a forgiving heart.

The first principle we must activate for healing and deliverance to be received is the act of forgiveness. It is the lynchpin that opens the flow of freedom into your life. You can be prayed over, have hands laid upon you, and even have words of knowledge declared over you concerning the situations you are facing. However, forgiveness is the key that opens the door for the manifestation of deliverance. I have seen many people receive their freedom on the heels of extending forgiveness to those who offended them.

I refer to forgiveness as an act that unlocks blessing. The reason I refer to it as an act is because it is not based on feelings or emotions. Forgiveness is determined by a deliberate, willful action of choosing to release offense or hurt. It is an act that is accomplished by faith, and not by sight or feelings.

Job's Act of Forgiveness

In the previous chapter, I specifically mentioned the account of Job and the restoration he experienced. Clearly, there was a tremendous amount of emotional and physical pain that he encountered. Anytime you think that you are really going through a tough situation, I encourage you to read the book of Job. To say that he went through difficulty is a mild statement in comparison to all he experienced.

Job lost his family, his health, and all his possessions in a short amount of time. It was very traumatic. Most people would not have responded in the same way that Job did. The Bible specifically says that he did not sin with his lips, nor did he charge God falsely. He did not blame God for the adversity of his life.

Not only did Job refuse to blame the Lord, but he did not blame those around him. He refrained from venting his frustration and pain upon others. His friends pointed their collective finger at him, but he refused to do the same. Job did not play the "blame game."

The Folly of Blaming

It seems that when people go through challenging times, they often point their finger at God as if He is the one sending the problems they are facing. Even those who say they do not believe in the Lord will cry out, "*Why, God?*" When people have their backs up against the wall, they look for someone to blame. Rarely do they look in the mirror. The problem with blaming

God is that you will not be able to come through the situation while you are pointing the finger at the only one who has the power to deliver you. This blame-shifting will also prevent you from walking in true forgiveness. Think about it!

As Job was going through his adversity, his friends gathered around him to "comfort" him. Unfortunately, they did everything but comfort him and spoke a bunch of foolishness. They made inaccurate claims against Job and the Lord as they poured gasoline on a fire of pain that was already burning in Job's life.

At the end of the story, God rebukes them for everything that they spoke falsely.

> And so it was, after the LORD had spoken these words to Job, that the LORD said to Eliphaz the Temanite, "My wrath is aroused against you and your two friends, for you have not spoken of Me what is right, as My servant Job has. Now therefore, take for yourselves seven bulls and seven rams, go to My servant Job, and offer up for yourselves a burnt offering; and My servant Job shall pray for you. For I will accept him, lest I deal with you according to your folly; because you have not spoken of Me what is right, as My servant Job has" (Job 42:7-8).

God justified Job but rebuked his friends for speaking foolishly. God was not angry at them for gathering around Job in their attempts to comfort him, rather for the words of their mouth that charged and blamed both Job and the Lord.

Restoration requires that we speak the right thing. Words of foolishness spoken will open the door for the enemy to wreak havoc. We must guard what we hear and say during times when our faith is being tried. We will speak in more detail concerning this in a future chapter.

Repentance is Necessary

The interesting aspect that starts the entire process of turnaround in Job's life is found in the verse preceding God's rebuke of his friends.

> "I have heard of You by the hearing of the ear, but now my eye sees You. Therefore I abhor myself, And repent in dust and ashes" (Job 42:5-6).

One thing we observe that Job did to start his turnaround and restoration is he repented. He acknowledged his wrong and changed his perspective. Job confessed to saying things that he did not understand and declaring things out of his own ignorance.

This is something that happens frequently with believers when painful things happen in their lives. They respond with words flowing from the emotional trauma of the moment. These words are usually knee-jerk reactions that are absent of biblical truth. Unfortunately, this only empowers a dire situation to become worse.

Turnaround Begins with Turning Around

It is important to understand that a turnaround in our life cannot begin until we first turn around. Many people are expecting things to change without them doing anything different. However, I have found that change happens when the change starts with us. We must be willing to change the way we think, believe, and speak. We must be willing to change the things we have been doing and ways that we have conducted our lives. Remember, the definition of insanity is to keep doing the same thing while expecting different results.

Job asked God to forgive him. He received forgiveness in areas where he had fallen short. He made the adjustments in his life that needed to be made. This catapulted him into a season of restoration, a divine *SHALAM* experience.

On the heels of Job's repentance, we see a beautiful picture of a sacrifice being made for sin. This makes way for the blessing to be released. Immediately following the sacrifice being made, we read this:

> And the LORD restored Job's losses when he prayed for his friends. Indeed, the LORD gave Job twice as much as he had before (Job 42:10).

Notice the sequence that happens: Job repents, his friends repent and make sacrifices, and then Job prays for his friends. Job forgives and blesses those who spoke wrongly about him and to him. He did not become bitter and angry. He chose to forgive those who sinned against him. Job received forgiveness and he forgave others.

It would have been quite easy for him to become bitter against his friends after their false charges. Let us call it what it is: lying about him. He could have given them the cold shoulder and told them to get out of his face. There are numerous responses that Job could have engaged in justifiably. However, he chose to do what was right, walk in love, and forgive those who wronged him.

Job Enacted Restoration

Many people read the book of Job as a story of pain and suffering. However, it is much more a guidebook to experiencing God's restorative power within our lives. It reveals things that we can enact to see God move and restore on the other side of adversity and pain.

We must understand that we live in a fallen world and things happen to everyone. Many times, we do not know why. Sometimes it makes no sense. However, we can be confident that we serve a God who will restore. He is *Jehovah-SHALAM*!

Just like Job chose to forgive, we must do the same. Regardless of what happened or what they did, forgiveness is a choice we must make. We do not forgive because we feel like it; we forgive because it is the right thing to do, and Jesus commanded it.

The reality is that when you initially forgive others, most of the time, you will not feel anything other than the pain, hurt, or anger that first accompanied the offense. In the beginning stages of forgiveness, the act itself can sometimes only bring to your remembrance the things that happened. However, forgiveness must be articulated and stated for it to be realized within your life.

Failure to Forgive Keeps Us Imprisoned

The failure to forgive others will keep you bound to that experience. The person who hurt you will continue to do so in your mind for as long as you hold on to the experience. You enable the individual who offended you to continue doing the same thing repeatedly. Failure to forgive others causes you to constantly relive the negative experiences that hurt you.

Please understand this important principle: If we do not forgive, we will be imprisoned by offense and hurt. It will cause torment within our own lives and eventually the lives of others. We will end up doing the same thing to the people we love that was wrongly done to us. The hurt and pain we carry will become the motivators of our actions displayed to others. This becomes the old cliche in operation: "hurt people, hurt people."

Living in the Pattern of Another's Sin

Jesus said, "*Whoever's sins you retain, they are retained by you*," which means that the sins we fail to forgive will be acted out by us. This is the reason that we see so often that those who have been abused become the next generation of abusers. Those who have been mistreated become the next generation to mistreat others. It is a vicious cycle that can only be broken through the power of forgiveness. It can happen in no other way!

The truth is that if we fail to forgive, we will live in the pattern of another person's sin against us. Their action becomes the imprint that establishes our future behavior and conduct. Everything that we hated, we become. We become the perpetrators of the same action that hurt us. However, we end up doing it to those who are closest to us. This is the danger of failing to forgive others.

Jesus Taught Us to Forgive

Jesus spoke about the importance of forgiveness. He was not silent on this matter. He emphasized it numerous times in various contexts. Most believers want to pull these Scripture verses out when they need forgiveness. However, they are not quick to do the same when they have been wronged.

> And forgive us our debts, As we forgive our debtors. And do not lead us into temptation, But deliver us from the evil one. For Yours is the kingdom and the power and the glory forever. Amen. "For if you forgive men their trespasses, your heavenly Father will also forgive you. But if you do not forgive men their trespasses, neither will your Father forgive your trespasses" (Matthew 6:12-15).

Jesus' disciples asked Him to teach them to pray. One of the six specific things that Jesus mentioned in His instruction was to both receive and extend forgiveness. The previous Scripture is the last half of Jesus' teaching on prayer, but it is easily observed how much emphasis He places on forgiveness. When you think of the different things that Jesus could have instructed His disciples to pray, it becomes apparent that forgiveness was a priority in His mind and heart.

Although the Lord's Prayer is all-encompassing, we realize through Jesus' instruction that forgiveness is an imperative element: it is not optional. When we look at Jesus' other teachings on forgiveness, we understand that it is necessary for this principle to be enacted for prayer to be answered. The failure to forgive will cause a roadblock to answered prayer. Jesus said that it causes a person to become unforgiven by the Father. Wow, think about it!

The bottom line is we can choose to obey the words of Jesus and forgive, or we can choose to disobey and hold on to our pain. Choosing to forgive will bring restoration and life. Choosing to maintain a held offense will produce death and destruction. What do you desire?

I encourage you to obey the words of Jesus. This is the key to restoration. God will arise on your behalf, and He will restore all that the enemy stole from you. He is *Jehovah-SHALAM* and will manifest His power as you make the choice to forgive. Do it today!

3

Forgiveness—Avoiding Destruction

> And Absalom spoke to his brother Amnon neither good nor bad. For Absalom hated Amnon, because he had forced his sister Tamar (2 Samuel 13:22).

Forgiveness is the key to restoration; it unlocks heaven's best for you. However, failure to forgive produces the opposite; it opens the gates of hell to destroy your life and family. You must understand that unforgiveness will destroy you. It will wreak havoc in your home, marriage, career, and church life. It causes incorrect perceptions of others and judgment of their motives. Our perceptions become tainted because of the filter we carry and use—the filter of unforgiveness.

I want to share with you a biblical account of how an individual with great promise and destiny was assassinated by his own failure to forgive. His inability to release a hurtful action caused him to spiral down a rabbit hole to a place of self-destruction.

Absalom's Unforgiveness

Absalom was the son of King David. He had a bright future ahead of him. The Bible specifically speaks of him as being handsome. I am sure he could have chosen any single woman in the kingdom of Israel for his wife. He was an heir to the throne, a prince of the kingdom. However, one tragic event that was mishandled by him changed his trajectory dramatically.

When we read the account of Absalom, we see the event which led to his demise. His sister, Tamar, was raped by his half-brother, Amnon (2 Samuel 13). Tamar told Absalom what happened. He, in turn, told his sister to keep it to herself and not take it to heart. However, Absalom allowed offense and unforgiveness to direct his life from that time forward. Everything we read that took place in Absalom's life from that point was dictated by the embrace of offense and failure to forgive. He became a marionette on strings controlled by the Puppet Master named Unforgiveness and Bitterness.

When Everything Went Wrong

Absalom told his sister to brush off what happened to her (not to be offended). He told her to forget about it. However, he did the exact opposite, walking in unforgiveness and becoming bitter. This was the process that sent Absalom down the road of destruction.

Jesus said that if your brother offends you, go to him. He also said to love your enemy. Absalom refused to speak to his brother at all and hated him. Absalom cultivated a root of bitterness within his heart. He fertilized the seeds of offense by refusing to talk to Amnon. Jesus commanded us to forgive, but Absalom allowed his hatred to grow as he continued to walk in unforgiveness. The root of bitterness was planted so deep within Absalom's life that two years later, he murdered

Amnon. He became a worse sinner than his brother, the rapist. Think about it!

Time Makes It Worse

There was a two-year lapse between the time Tamar was raped and the murder of his brother. Absalom could have been working on forgiving Amnon. However, he began plotting on the day his sister was raped.

> … for only Amnon is dead. For by the command of Absalom this has been determined from the day that he forced his sister Tamar (2 Samuel 13:32b).

Absalom had already planned and plotted the murder of Amnon from day one. For two years, he meditated on it. The voice of offense spoke to him daily and gave him justification for his plot to murder his brother. For two years, he planned it. For two years, he fantasized about Amnon's blood being spilled. Finally, at the right moment, his plan was hatched.

For two years, Absalom could have been working to remove the offense. For two years, he could have been declaring forgiveness. For two years, he could have been having a dialogue with his brother. However, he chose to embrace the vicious cycle of offense, unforgiveness, and bitterness. He opened the door for the enemy, and the devil obliged him.

Double the Sinner

This story is tragic. Absalom was a prince in the kingdom of Israel. He was in line for the throne. However, he forfeited his purpose and destiny because he failed to forgive his brother. Absalom gave his ear over to the voice of offense, which produced bitterness and hatred. This culminated in the murder of his brother.

Everything that God destined Absalom to become in the kingdom of Israel was flushed down the toilet. It was not because of something done to him personally; he took the offense of his sister and would not forgive his brother. Absalom's anger was understandable, yet that did not make anything he did right. Someone may have a natural justification for being angry, but it will never justify unforgiveness and bitterness. That is the road to disaster.

Later in Absalom's life, he became twice the sinner. While his half-brother had raped his sister, Absalom raped all of his father's concubines and had sex with them in plain view of the nation.

> So they pitched a tent for Absalom on the top of the house, and Absalom went in to his father's concubines in the sight of all Israel (2 Samuel 16:22).

The very thing that Absalom abhorred Amnon for doing, raping a family member, he did to a greater degree in front of the nation. Absalom was empowered and justified by the voice of offense to which he was heeding. The voice that promised him revenge is the voice that robbed him of his destiny. The voice that promised to even the score caused him to be the loser.

Forgive and Refrain

Again, Jesus said, "If you forgive the sins of any, they are forgiven them; if you retain the sins of any, they are retained" (John 20:23). Jesus was not giving His disciples power to forgive people of their sins. Rather, He was articulating a spiritual principle at work. That principle is when you choose to forgive, that sin is released from you. Forgiveness will shut the mouth of offense and keep you from repeating the same action. The act of forgiveness disables sin from reproducing both in and through you.

However, when you choose to walk in unforgiveness, you retain that sin and give place for the offense to be repeated by you. This voice will become increasingly louder to the point that you will be deafened to the voice of the Holy Spirit. The sin you retain is the open door for the enemy to build a stronghold within your life. This is what Absalom allowed to happen in his own life.

Eventually, he was destroyed. His father, David, wept at the news of his death. Absalom's demise was self-inflicted. He brought it upon himself through an open door called unforgiveness. Many believe Absalom's demise was because he led a rebellion. However, the rebellion was merely a manifestation of his failure to forgive. His sin did not begin as a rebellion; it began through unforgiveness. The root of the rebellion he led against his own father, David, was rooted in embracing an offense. He held on to it and would not release it. Think about it!

Patterns Repeated and Poison Drank

One of the primary things that we observe in the account of Absalom is that the failure to forgive causes one to repeat the same destructive patterns. He repeated the very thing that he abhorred in his brother, Amnon. I have seen this happen before in the lives of well-meaning Christians. The hurt and pain that they could not release became the very thing that patterned their behavior. It was not intentional, but their intentions made it no less real. Unforgiveness drove them down an undesired path, but the control it had in their lives caused them to do the very things they despised.

When anyone retains and holds onto the sins or offenses of another person, their behavior and conduct will be augmented. It is as if there is a force controlling them to behave in an unseemly manner. Many times, they will attempt to modify these patterns in their lives, but it is to no avail because of their neglect to release it, let it go, and forgive.

Unforgiveness is equivalent to drinking poison while expecting someone else to die. The truth is that choosing not to forgive is poison to your system: spirit, soul, and body. You are the only one who dies. It will produce negative effects in every area of your life. We must resist this with everything in our being.

The Punishment of Unforgiveness

Jesus gave a parable concerning the importance of forgiveness and what happens when someone fails to do so. He spoke of a servant who was forgiven of a large debt that he owed. However, that same servant refused to forgive his fellow servant of a minuscule debt that was owed to him. He punished him as he demanded to be repaid. This is what Jesus said was the outcome of that servant.

> "Then his master, after he had called him, said to him, 'You wicked servant! I forgave you all that debt because you begged me. Should you not also have had compassion on your fellow servant, just as I had pity on you?' And his master was angry, and delivered him to the torturers until he should pay all that was due to him. So My heavenly Father also will do to you if each of you, from his heart, does not forgive his brother his trespasses" (Matthew 18:32-35).

We can see from this parable that the Lord is serious concerning the act of forgiveness. Jesus clearly communicated that anyone who refuses to forgive will be turned over to torturers. Wow! Think about that for a moment. Jesus said that you will be tortured if you do not forgive your brother.

Failure to Forgive Will Torture

When I think about that statement, it is somewhat frightening. I have always disdained any kind of horror movie. The sight of anyone being tortured, even if it is in a movie, makes me physically sick and nauseated. I am repulsed when I read of anyone who has been through any kind of torturous situation. So, the very thought of being tortured because of the failure to forgive should make us choose to release our offense and bitterness against anyone quickly.

Jesus was not attempting to produce fear in our hearts with the threat of what could happen to us. However, He was emphasizing the severity of the spiritual dynamics that take place when someone chooses to walk in unforgiveness. As I said earlier and now repeat, failure to forgive others is like us drinking poison while expecting them to die. Unfortunately, you are the only person hurt.

There are many Christians today who are being spiritually and emotionally tortured. We usually want to point the finger and blame someone else for the pain that we are suffering. However, much of the suffering we experience is self-induced. God is not the author, and neither is the devil, in these types of situations. It is self-inflicted pain caused by the unwillingness to forgive. The only way to remove this type of torture is to release the offense.

Scientifically Proven

It has been proven scientifically that emotional bitterness and resentment can cause physical disease to manifest in your body. Remember that unforgiveness is at the root of all bitterness. Here are some excerpts from an article written by Dr. Debi Silber concerning the effects of bitterness:

> Resentment and bitterness are like toxic fuel for stress... This constant state of stress can lead to a host of physical issues, including high blood pressure, increased heart rate, and a weakened immune system. … chronic bitterness and resentment can weaken your body's ability to fight off infections and illnesses… Resentment and bitterness can raise your blood pressure, which is a significant risk factor for heart disease and stroke… Emotions

> like resentment and bitterness can wreak havoc on your sleep patterns… making it difficult to relax and fall asleep.
>
> Holding onto resentment and bitterness can disrupt the delicate balance of your digestive system. Stress-induced changes in gut function can lead to gastrointestinal problems like irritable bowel syndrome (IBS), indigestion, and acid reflux… Emotional tension can manifest physically in the form of muscle stiffness and pain. ...Over time, it can severely impact your mobility and overall quality of life…
>
> Possibly one of the most surprising physical dangers of resentment and bitterness is its potential to accelerate the aging process. Chronic stress, driven by these negative emotions, can lead to premature aging of the skin… (Silberman,"7 Physical Dangers of Resentment and Bitterness").

This Affects Every Part of Your Being

So, unforgiveness can do more than just affect your spirit and soul; it can negatively affect your body. My friend, it is not worth it. It is time to lay it down. Why should you allow the individual who hurt you to continue to do so every day of your life? Forgiveness is better.

I recognize this can be difficult. I understand that the pain you experienced may be unbearable. Perhaps the wrong was committed against a close family member, a spouse, son, or daughter. Those things are extremely painful to walk through. What I am sharing about forgiveness is not minimizing what happened or what you experienced. However, it will only continue to haunt and torture you if there is a failure to embrace forgiveness.

As a father, I have said before, "You can do what you want to me, but don't mess with my family." I am sure this sentiment is echoed by fathers and mothers everywhere. So, whenever someone does something to hurt or harm our spouse or children, it is incredibly challenging to overcome. We feel as though to forgive them is to betray our family. This is unthinkable to most people who love their families. Therefore, we hang on to that offense in the name of loving those who are dearest to us.

The only way we can forgive in these types of situations is to receive God's empowering grace and then forgive by faith. We do not forgive based on feelings; we do it as an act of our will. It is a process. This means that from the point you first verbalize forgiveness, there will be a period of time until it is realized emotionally. Forgiveness is usually not felt immediately. However, just because you fail to feel forgiveness does not mean that you have not forgiven someone. This is so important to know.

Forgiveness Is for Our Benefit

Understand that the forgiveness we extend to others is not for their benefit, but for ours. The person that you choose to hold a grudge against will not be hurt by your failure to forgive. However, you will continue to suffer if you do not forgive.

Forgiveness benefits the one who is forgiving, not the one being forgiven.

One of the greatest misunderstandings that people possess concerning forgiveness is its equivalency to forgetting. The truth is they are two different things. Forgetting is not the prerequisite for forgiveness. There is no guarantee that you will ever forget something solely because you forgive. Typically, you do not.

Forgiveness merely means that you are choosing to release it and let it go. You will hold no negative judgment against the person who caused the pain. You choose to do this because it costs you more to hold on than to let go!

My Story

Many years ago, in the beginning season of our ministry, a minister spoke some things falsely about me. The things he said prevented me from being employed by a church that was desiring me to become their music director. When I found out what he said, I was shocked and hurt. Soon that hurt turned to anger.

When I told my parents what happened, they were enraged. My father was ready to visit this minister while being accompanied by a baseball bat. He was visibly upset. I spoke with my father, and I told him that God would work it out while a multitude of emotions were running through me at the moment.

At that time, my wife, Stacey, and I were walking through a season of transition. We had a two-year-old son, Joshua, and we were living with my parents as we sought direction for our lives and ministry. When this took place, I felt dejected, hopeless, fearful, sad, and angry all at the same time. Neither Stacey nor I knew what to do other than trust God to supernaturally open a door of opportunity for us.

Forgiveness Realized

Several months later, God opened a supernatural door with a neighboring church and ministry. It was located not far (about fifteen miles) from the church where I was previously employed. For a time, I had to drive by this church numerous times during the week. Every time I drove by the church building, something would arise within me. Unfortunately, it was not the Spirit of the Lord. Truthfully, there was still hurt, anger, and resentment in my heart that was slowly turning to bitterness.

One day, as I was driving by this church building, the Lord spoke to me. He told me, "*Every time you drive by here, extend your hand and say, 'I forgive and release you.'*" So, I started doing that. It was difficult at first. However, the more I did it, the easier it got. Several months later, I noticed that I drove by the building and did not even realize it. I knew then that forgiveness had been totally realized within my heart.

The gnawing in my gut was no longer there. The feelings of resentment had disappeared. It was no longer something that haunted or tormented me. I had overcome offense, unforgiveness, and bitterness because I had chosen to forgive.

You Cannot Wait for an Apology

About six months later, I had lunch with the pastor who spoke against me. During our meal, he apologized to me for what he had said. I expressed that I received his apology. The reality was that I had already forgiven him months before because I could not afford to wait for a formal apology from him. I could not afford to drink the poison of unforgiveness for six months. It would have killed me.

The Lord taught me valuable lessons throughout this process that I have carried with me in my life and ministry. The importance of forgiveness is the primary thing, more than any other. If you choose to forgive, you will come out on the other side of the challenge with victory. If you get sour and bitter, you will end up with nothing but more pain and suffering. What do you want? The choice is yours!

Taking Action

You may be at a place right now where you need to forgive and release some offense within your life. It begins with you articulating it—saying it aloud. It may not be easy at first. However, making the declaration of forgiveness empowers it within your life. Death and life are in the power of the tongue.

Sometimes, it may help to make a list. Ask the Holy Spirit to illuminate any person that you need to forgive. If there is a gnawing in your gut when you see certain people, then the chances are that forgiveness needs to be extended.

Forgiveness does not require that you call or contact the individual who may have wronged you. This is not necessarily an issue between you and them, as much as you and the Lord. I always recommend that before people attempt to reconcile, they forgive one another first. Reconciliation has no chance where forgiveness is not first rendered.

Choose today to forgive. This is the first step for healing and deliverance. Release all the negative feelings and emotions that you have been carrying. Refuse to allow the hurt of yesterday to keep you from experiencing the destiny God has for your future. Choose to be set free from that which may be tormenting you. Let it begin with the act of forgiveness.

Forgiveness Exercise

Here is a five-step forgiveness exercise for you to do.

1. Spend a moment in prayer and ask the Lord to reveal to you anyone who has wronged, hurt, or spoken evil of you or whom you are bitter toward in any way.

2. Write down their names and what they did that caused the hurt and pain.

3. Articulate forgiveness—speak it out—over every one of the names. Speak their name and what you are forgiving them for doing to you. Say, "*I forgive (name) for (offense).*" Remember, you forgive by faith, not by your feelings.

4. Declare and speak blessing over them. Pray that God would bless them.

5. Refuse to talk negatively about them from this point forward. Cast it away from your thinking by the power of the Holy Spirit.

4

Don't Live as a Victim

> And Joseph said to his brothers, "Please come near to me." So they came near. Then he said: "I am Joseph your brother, whom you sold into Egypt. But now, do not therefore be grieved or angry with yourselves because you sold me here; for God sent me before you to preserve life... But as for you, you meant evil against me; but God meant it for good, in order to bring it about as it is this day, to save many people alive. Now therefore, do not be afraid; I will provide for you and your little ones." And he comforted them and spoke kindly to them (Genesis 45:4-5; 50:20-21).

There are many believers today who fail to walk in the victory they have been given through Christ Jesus. They live defeated and downtrodden solely because of their perceptions of their past experiences and plights. A picture has been painted on the canvas of their hearts and minds of pain and hurt, where they are always coming up on the short end of the stick. They see themselves as victims in a world that hates them, and sometimes, they even feel as though God is a part of the problem.

Understand this: It is impossible to walk in victory while living as a victim. To live as an overcomer in Christ, one must ditch the "woe is me" disposition. Victory cannot be realized while wallowing in self-pity and fatalism. It is impossible to live triumphantly while holding to the beliefs of a victim. Let me say it in street language: You cannot be a winner while thinking like a loser.

Many Christians are paralyzed in life solely because they believe they are victims. They are persuaded they have been dealt a bad hand of cards and are doomed to fail. They do not believe that there is anything they can do other than suffer through the pain as they traverse their earthly existence. Regardless of what they do, their fate is sealed, and they are doomed while here on Earth.

Jesus Liberated Us

Nothing is farther from the truth for any Christian. Jesus liberated us from any and all power that satan had within our lives. Demonic principalities and authorities have been destroyed, and the devil has no leverage over us. He whom the Son sets free is free indeed!

The truth is that we are victors in Christ, regardless of any past experience. The truth is that we have been given the power to overcome every situation and circumstance by the power of the blood of Jesus. These truths are greater than any negative painful thing that we have experienced. It trumps anything that anyone has ever said to demean our personage. The truth of

God's Word is greater than it all. This is what we must believe and allow to permeate every crevice of our minds and hearts.

The Example of Joseph

Let us examine the life of Joseph and the things he endured. He experienced betrayal, pain, slavery, false accusations, and wrongful imprisonment. Yet, at the end of the story, Joseph overcame it all.

The account of Joseph that we read in the Bible is an amazing story. It is an example of how a man of covenant overcame numerous obstacles and challenges to see God's promise fulfilled. God had made a promise to his great-grandfather, Abraham. He declared that his seed would be blessed and mighty upon the earth. God promised to bless the children and offspring of Abraham, which means God promised to bless Joseph.

In the house of Jacob (Israel), there were twelve sons. Joseph was favored above them all. Unfortunately, this resulted in great envy and jealousy arising within the hearts of his brothers. They despised him and wanted to get rid of him. So, they created a pit, captured Joseph, and threw him into it. They told their elderly father that a wild animal had killed him. Jacob wept bitterly and was broken-hearted.

Joseph's brothers then sold him into slavery. He went to Egypt where he excelled in the house of Potiphar. After a sexual advance was made by Potiphar's wife, Joseph ran away to prevent sinning. Potiphar's wife lied and said that Joseph attempted to rape her. For that, he was thrown in prison.

Bad Attitudes Are Easy to Develop

Let us stop here for a moment. It would have been so easy for Joseph to develop a bad attitude at this juncture. He could have easily developed a "woe is me" disposition; anybody would be tempted to do so in these circumstances. However, Joseph refused to see himself as a victim of others, even though he had genuinely been victimized. Joseph chose to think and believe differently.

Continuing with the story, Joseph later became the chief of the prison. The captain trusted him and realized that God was with him. When the butler and baker of Pharaoh each had a dream, Joseph interpreted the dreams, and it happened just as he said. He only requested that the butler remember him, but unfortunately, Joseph was forgotten. Think about it. How easy he could have said, "*Forget this. I'm not going to interpret anyone else's dream!*" However, he did not.

Then, a day came when Pharaoh had a dream that needed interpretation, and Joseph was remembered and called upon. He interpreted the dream and was immediately released from prison and promoted to a position of power.

Let me go over this sequence of events. From the PIT to POTIPHAR'S to PROPOSITIONED to PRISON to PASSED OVER and forgotten. Then, eventually, he was PROMOTED and given POSITION and POWER.

Things Happen

At any point in time, Joseph could have allowed the mistreatment from others to form a victim mentality within him. However, he refused to allow the injurious behavior of others to define him. He rose above it all because he recognized that God was with him.

The reality is that things happen to all of us. There is no one living on this earth that has not experienced pain. We have all traversed through hurt administered through others. No one is exempt from these things. Welcome to Earth.

The difference between those who rise above it and those who succumb is their perspective. You can choose to see yourself as a helpless victim or as one who has been given the power to overcome. Your choice will determine what you become. Choosing to perceive yourself as an overcomer will empower you to rise above the pain. Choosing to let the actions of others define you will cause you to sink.

Pointing the Finger

It would have been easy for Joseph to point his finger at those who were oppressing him. He had the opportunity to use them as his excuse for the rest of his life. He had the right to blame them for his plight, though this would have only led to him dying in prison. Instead, he recognized that God was for him; therefore, no one could be against him.

If we live pointing our finger at others, we forfeit our deliverance and promotion. Blaming others is an indicator that we are still hanging on to painful things from the past. Even though there may be no hateful feelings toward the one who administered the hurt, if we blame them for where we are presently, we have not fully forgiven and released them. We are tied to the things of the past because of the blame that we continue to shovel in their direction.

It is important to take forgiveness beyond the place of articulating the words, "*I forgive you.*" This is where it starts, but it is not the final destination of the process. We must release those individuals from the responsibility of the actions that negatively affected us. If we fail to do so, we will spend the rest of our lives pointing the finger from the place of a victim. This is no way to live. It is not a place of victory and will result in the forfeiture of our restoration.

Lay It Down

To live victorious requires us to lay down the things that hurt us. It requires that we move beyond the pain into the place Jesus spoke of, where "nothing will by any means hurt you!" Victorious living cannot coexist with living as a victim. It is utterly impossible because the two are diametrically opposed to one another.

If you are pointing the finger, you are living as a victim; and if you live as a victim, you will live defeated. This is the reason we must rid ourselves of any form of a victim mentality. It is your enemy just like sin, sickness, poverty, and oppression. It does not come from God; it originates in the heart of satan. Refuse to be held captive by this wicked and deceptive spirit.

Going back to the account of Joseph, we see that he did not point his finger at his brothers. He did not rehearse the pain that he had experienced in the pit and Potiphar's house. He did not recount the false accusations that resulted in him being imprisoned. We read that Joseph not only forgave his brothers but credited them with being the hand of God to bring salvation to their family. Let that sink in for a moment.

God Can Turn Things Around

Could it be that God can turn around what others meant for your evil and work it for your good? Is it possible that God is greater than those who would seek to harm you? Can God reverse things and work it for your favor and promotion? The answer to all these questions is a resounding, "YES!"

When we experienced Hurricane Michael in 2018, God took what the enemy meant for evil and worked it for our good. It was a devastating event that I would never desire for anyone to experience, but God turned it around and we ended up with more than we had before.

It would have been easy for us to get upset and angry after such a horrific storm. We could have pointed our finger and blamed God for the devastation, and some people did. However, I understood that pointing the finger, blaming God, and becoming a victim would only worsen the situation. It was imperative that we look to God as our Restorer and not accuse and blame Him for being the destroyer.

In these types of situations, it is easy to succumb to the voice of emotion that is screaming in your ear. It is easy to question if you did something wrong to deserve your plight. All of us must contend with these things that shout loudly at us in moments of conflict and crisis. However, yielding to these voices will only lead to living as a victim. There is no victory when you live in that manner. You forsake and forfeit your own deliverance when these things take control of your thinking.

From Pain to Promotion

I shared a personal testimony in the previous chapter where I had to forgive someone who did some hurtful things to me. As I look back on it, I can truthfully say that God used what this individual did to prevent me from going the wrong direction. The result was a perfect alignment with God's plan and purpose for my life and ministry. At the time it happened, I felt my world had ended. However, the truth is my world was just starting on a new and brighter path.

God turned my pain into promotion. What I originally perceived as a setback was only used as a setup for blessing. I went through many emotional battles for several months; there was a war in my mind and emotions. However, I chose victory over victimization. I chose to believe God was greater and that my life was in His hands—it could not be controlled by what other people did to me.

We can live as a victim of the actions of others, or we can live as overcomers because of the actions of Christ. It is entirely up to us. One is the pathway of continued heartache and destruction while the other is the road of victory and triumph. What do you want? Make the right choice!

The Battle in the Mind

The account of Joseph is one of the most amazing stories in the Bible. However, the giant that he faced was not like Goliath standing on a battlefield that David faced. It was not natural walls that were insurmountable like Joshua encountered at Jericho. Neither was it like the prophets of Baal that Elijah challenged on Mount Carmel.

Joseph's battle was much bigger and greater. It was the internal battle within his mind and heart that raged after repeatedly being victimized by those that he both loved and served. He battled against the feelings of betrayal by his own flesh and blood, along with the people he served faithfully in Egypt. However, he overcame and never allowed himself to become a victim.

It is interesting to note that all the accounts we read in the Bible were specifically written to be an example for us (James 5:10-11). Some are there to expose what not to do. Others are there to reveal biblical principles in action that will cause success and blessing to be released within our lives. Then there are those where encouragement is found as we witness God's ability to lift His people above painful experiences and cause them to triumph. They give us hope and a joyful expectation that if He did it for them, He will do it again!

If you have a difficult day, just consider Joseph for a moment. If you think the world is out to get you, read again what Joseph said to the very ones who betrayed him and sold him into slavery. If you believe there is no way out of your predicament, consider the end of Joseph and how he was promoted to a position of power! Hallelujah!

The Manifestation of Unbelief

Most people do not realize that living as a victim is a manifestation of unbelief. It is a postured declaration that one believes that God is not greater than those they feel have harmed them. Living as a victim minimizes the God you serve and magnifies the ability of others to lord over you.

I recognize that this may not be easy to hear if someone has victimized you in the past. However, as long as your experience is magnified more than the power and ability of God, you will remain stuck in the place that someone else created for you. God did not put you there. He made you more than a conqueror. Jesus created a way out. Choose the pathway of healing and refuse to continue in the pain of yesterday.

The Culture of Victimization

Unfortunately, we are baptized daily in a culture that makes heroes of those who have been victimized. I understand why this has happened. For so long, people who hurt others have not been held accountable. As a result, there has been a cry for justice from those who have genuinely been harmed. The pain they have carried is crying out for acknowledgment and accountability.

Let me first say that I sympathize with those who have been harmed by anyone, especially those who experienced it at the hands of those in places of authority who wrongfully leveraged themselves for their own selfish purposes. Those who have done such things should be held accountable for the wrong they have committed. Justice is a part of the character of God, just like mercy. Justice should be rendered for reasons of acknowledgment and accountability, while mercy should be extended for the purposes of forgiveness and restoration.

With this said, we must understand that the continual drone of voices shouting out their victimization has harmed much more than it has helped. It has shaped a mentality in our culture and in the Church that has trapped people in past experiences. It is a line of thinking that causes many to remain victims within the prison of their minds.

False Victims

When people live as victims, a word of correction may often be perceived as rejection, and thus they are irreparably harmed. Many years ago, there was an individual who was the head of a department within our church on a volunteer basis. He posted something on social media that I believed was inappropriate. I called the individual and asked him to remove the post and gave reasons why it should be removed. At first, he questioned and argued. I finally told him that his post did not represent the values of the church, nor my values. He reluctantly took the post down.

In about two weeks, he left our church. Then he began making YouTube® videos where he talked about abusive leadership in the church and insinuated that I was one of those abusive leaders. The things he said about me (while he never actually called my name) were blatantly false. Unfortunately, people knew where he went to church previously and rightly concluded that he was talking about me.

So, where did all of this begin to go south? It was when I asked him to remove a Facebook® post. I suddenly became abusive and controlling simply because he (a department head within our church) posted something I believed to be inappropriate. He felt that an abusive leader victimized him because he was asked to accurately reflect the values of our church body. This individual became a false victim because of things he fabricated in his own mind.

False Accusations of Abuse

Think about this: Since when does asking someone not to say or post something questionable fall into the category of abuse? However, this is the way our "victim culture" now defines abuse. The thinking is, "*If I don't like it, then I'm being abused.*" The unfortunate thing is that every time they cry abuse in these types of situations, it minimizes the pain of those who are being abused. Let that sink in for a moment!

It must be understood that when a person who claims to be a victim makes a false accusation against someone, they victimize the person they are accusing. Unfortunately, this happens far too often. The person claiming to be abused becomes the abuser. Truthfully, I was the one victimized by an individual's fallacious stories that were then published on the internet. *Of course, we all know that anything published on the internet is the gospel truth* (sarcasm intended).

I chose to forgive this individual and move forward. I was not going to allow the things he said to determine my future. The only person that we should allow to dictate our future is Jesus and His voice. No other person should be given that power or authority within our lives.

This is the truth, regardless of what has happened to you, forgiveness is still required. You must release it and move forward. You cannot live in the frame of mind of being a victim. Allowing the tragic event that you experienced to linger will only prolong and reinforce your pain.

Your Rights vs. What Is Right

Consider again the account of Joseph. If anyone had a right to cry foul, he did. If anyone had a right to cry abuse, he most certainly did. If anyone had a right to say that he had been done wrong, Joseph could have shouted it from the mountaintops throughout the land. He had every right to sing "Another Somebody Done Somebody Wrong Song." However, he did not!

Though Joseph had a legitimate right to seek justice and retribution, he chose to show mercy. We could argue that it would have been justified if he had thrown his brothers in prison. Justice permitted and even required it. However, he chose to travel the road of mercy and forgiveness. Joseph understood that having a right to do something did not make it the right thing to do. Think about it!

Instead of crying foul, he said that what his brothers meant for evil had been turned around to work for good. Instead of saying he had been abused, he told his brothers not to be grieved or angry at themselves. He did not ever say to his brothers that he had been wronged. Instead, he comforted them and spoke kindly to them. He was more concerned for his brothers than some type of secret vindication. This blows my mind!

An Example to Follow

Every time I read the account of Joseph, I am awed. When I consider everything he went through yet maintained a right spirit, it causes me to be overwhelmed at the grace of God that worked in and through him. I am sure that he had moments of discouragement. I know that he felt the emotional pain of betrayal. However, at the end of the day, Joseph overcame it all by refusing to live as a victim. That same grace is available to us if we will allow God to work in our lives.

Let Joseph be an example for all of us. He was abused and mistreated but forgave and restored. He chose the path of restoration and freedom rather than victimization and bitterness.

You are not a victim; you are an overcomer. You are more than a conqueror and the devil is under your feet. God is for you, so who can be against you? Rise up today and be who God created you to be!

Overcoming the Victim Mentality Exercise

1. Say aloud, "I am a victor, not a victim!"

2. Write down anything that has made you believe you are a victim.

3. Lay your hand on the piece of paper and declare, "Today, this ends. I am released from the power of these experiences because I am redeemed by the blood of Jesus."

4. Wad the piece of paper up and throw it in the trash!

5. Make the declaration, "He who the Son sets free is free indeed. I am free!

6. Start praising God that you are more than a conqueror!

7. Continue to thank God and declare every day that you triumph—"Thanks be to God who always causes us to triumph!"

5

Family Issues and Spiritual DNA

> "You shall not make for yourself a carved image—any likeness of anything that is in heaven above, or that is in the earth beneath, or that is in the water under the earth; you shall not bow down to them nor serve them. For I, the LORD your God, am a jealous God, visiting the iniquity of the fathers upon the children to the third and fourth generations of those who hate Me, but showing mercy to thousands, to those who love Me and keep My commandments" (Exodus 20:4-6).

In this passage of Scripture, we see that there is a blessing established for serving the Lord. God declares that He will show mercy for thousands of generations to those committed to loving Him and keeping His commandments. Wow! Think about that. God promises to show His love, mercy, and compassion on thousands of generations.

Most people fail to realize the full effect that their actions have on their children and future generations. However, the Bible has something profound to say about it. If we could fully comprehend the effect our behavior has not only on us but generations to come, I am confident that most people would modify their behavior and make different choices.

It is important to realize that we are not merely living for ourselves. Our behavior will profoundly affect our children, grandchildren, and great-grandchildren. It does not stop there but continues. The things we do are seeds sown for a future harvest in our lives. However, that harvest is not only reaped in our own lives but the lives of our children, too!

Seed Time and Harvest

We have heard teachings concerning the biblical principle of seed time and harvest as it relates to financial giving. I am thankful for the revelation that was proclaimed concerning financial seed and the harvest that would be reaped on the other side of our faithfulness. However, the principle of seed time and harvest extends far beyond the realm of finances.

We must understand that everything we do is a seed that is sown for a future harvest. Every action and every word spoken become seeds sown that will eventually be harvested. The seeds of loving and obeying God that are sown will result in the harvest of God showing mercy to thousands of your generations. Likewise, the seed of idolatry and sinful living that is sown will yield a harvest of consequences for future generations.

When people fail to realize this principle, they live lawlessly without any fear of God. When people understand this principle, they will live circumspectly with the knowledge that their actions are seeds sown as a harvest for their children. This works in both a positive and negative manner according to what kind of seed is sown. The good seeds of obedience to God will produce a good harvest for your family and onward. The bad seeds of disobedience will produce a bad harvest for generations to come.

Noah—The Blessing of Obedience

We read in the Bible the account of a man named Noah. God used him to bring salvation to his family by building an ark. It was God's means of protecting both Noah and his family from the flood that covered the entire Earth. Every living thing died except those who were in the ark.

We historically observe from Scripture that a man's obedience to God brought salvation and deliverance to his entire family. Noah's sons, daughters, and in-laws were saved because he chose to believe and obey. They were the only ones on the entire planet who were saved. Only eight people went into the ark, and eight people came out once the waters subsided. One man's obedience afforded blessing and protection for generations to come. Later, they were the ones who would repopulate the entire planet. Think about it.

Just like Noah, when we choose to obey God, there is promised protection that is afforded to us and our families. There is blessing that is released upon us as we continue to obey the Lord and love Him with all our hearts.

Noah—The Curse of Sin

As we continue to read the story of Noah, we see a shift happen. God blessed the vineyard that Noah planted. From that vineyard, he made wine from the grapes and then became intoxicated, which caused Noah to exhibit behavior that was inappropriate and unwise. He misused God's blessing, and in doing so, he sinned.

Noah stripped naked in his tent, and his son, Ham, came into the tent and saw his father's nakedness. When Noah woke up from his drunken stupor, he pronounced a curse, but not over Ham. Noah cursed Canaan, Ham's son—his innocent grandson.

I want you to see this sequence clearly. The first sin was that of Noah, as he got plastered drunk and then lay naked. Then, the sin of Ham took place as he went into his father's tent while he was naked (many theologians believe that Ham committed a sinful sexual act with his father). Then, once Noah awoke, he pronounced a curse on Ham's son Canaan. It was the sin of Canaan's father and grandfather that opened the door for a curse to come on him. He did nothing to deserve it; he was innocent, yet he was cursed because of the behavior of his father and grandfather.

So, decades and centuries later, Canaan and his descendants settled and populated a land area. Can you guess what it was called? If you said, "Canaan," then you are right. His descendants became known as the Canaanites. They were sinful and wicked people. It became a land filled with sexual perversion and debauchery. Hundreds of years later, the Israelites are commissioned to go in and destroy them because their wickedness is so great.

Can you see how that one man's sin opened the door for generational curses to be released? Noah's moment of self-indulgence was a chain-reaction event. Just like his obedience brought a blessing, his disobedience produced a curse.

Sin Produced a Cataclysmic Shift

We can also see this principle enacted at the beginning of creation. Adam and Eve's sin plunged all mankind into a curse. The first murder is committed by their son, Cain, against his own brother, Abel. The sin of the parents opened the door for the enemy to manipulate their children. One of their sons became a murderer, and the other was murdered. What a tragedy. The curse of sin infiltrated all mankind from that point forward.

The entire Earth experienced a cataclysmic shift the moment that Adam and Eve sinned. Before the fall, there were no thorns and briars. There was no pain and suffering. Sickness and disease did not exist. However, once their sin was consummated, the door was opened that unleashed demonic activity of all sorts.

Adam and Eve released the curse on all their descendants. The reality is that every individual born from that point was set up to sin. God did not set them up, but Adam's sin did. His disobedience to God's command opened the door to all manner of destruction. The law of sin and death had free rein to take control of humanity because of one man's sin.

Ancestral Sin and the Curse

It is important to understand that the curse comes not only as the result of your sin, but also of your ancestors. That means the behavior and conduct of your parents and grandparents affect your life. Their sin opens the door for the curse to be empowered. This is not a negative confession or proclamation, nor is it an attempt to blame previous generations for your issues. It is merely a biblical truth that we must acknowledge and then biblically address.

One misconception people have is that identifying things which happened in previous generations is pointing the finger or, in some way, blaming them. Understand that **identification** is not an **accusation**. If we fail to identify the problem, we cannot arrive at a cure. It is especially important that we are transparent and truthful if we are going to arrive at a place of freedom and deliverance.

The good news is that through Jesus' redemptive work at Calvary, every curse can be canceled. We are not doomed for the rest of our lives because our grandfather sinned. We can appropriate the power of the blood of Jesus and see every curse of hell broken and destroyed. The curse of sin can be replaced with the blessing of the Lord.

> Christ has redeemed us from the curse of the law, having become a curse for us (for it is written, "CURSED IS EVERYONE WHO HANGS ON A TREE"), that the blessing of Abraham might come upon the Gentiles in Christ Jesus, that we might receive the promise of the Spirit through faith (Galatians 3:13-14).

Jesus came to Earth for the purpose of redeeming mankind. That means He paid the price so that we would no longer be the property of the enemy. His blood was the only thing that could pay the high price upon our heads. Jesus willingly laid down His life so that we could have His. It was the greatest exchange that has ever been known to man. He paid the price for every man, woman, boy, and girl. Think about it!

Why did He do it? He did it so we could walk free from the curse that was released by Adam. In the letter written to the Romans, Paul states that by one man (Adam), death entered, and now by one man (Jesus), eternal life has come (Romans 5). Jesus redeemed us so that the sins of all our ancestors—our family DNA going all the way back to Adam and Noah—would have no more power over our lives.

Redeemed From the Curse and New DNA

Being redeemed from the curse means that it no longer has power over us. The curse that came into the world because of Adam's sin and our forefathers' wrongdoing has been rendered powerless by the blood of Jesus. The spiritual family DNA that was passed down from the sins of previous generations has been replaced. We are now part of the family of God, and Jesus has replaced our spiritual DNA.

Once we are born again, eternal life replaces the old nature. We are more than forgiven; we are a new creation in Christ. The old nature has passed away, which means it is dead. All things become new the moment you receive Jesus. This means you have new spiritual DNA. The old is gone, and the new is alive.

Acknowledgment of this understanding causes it to be activated within our lives. We are more than sinners saved by grace. We are now the righteousness of God in Christ Jesus with the very DNA of Heaven. It courses through our spiritual veins and arteries. We have royal blood that now flows throughout our spirit man. We now carry the DNA of the Heavenly Father! Hallelujah!

Appropriated by Faith

Everything in the kingdom of God must be appropriated by faith, regardless of what it may be. Salvation is received by faith. Ephesians 2:8 says that by grace, you are saved BY FAITH. There is no other way to receive the gift of salvation. The greatest virtuous deeds in the world cannot purchase or merit the gift of eternal life. The only path to salvation is through faith—believing that Jesus was raised from the dead and confessing His Lordship within your life.

Likewise, we receive healing in the same manner. Healing is received by faith. Jesus repeatedly told people things like, "*As your faith is, so be it unto you.*" Jesus credited people's faith with the miracles that transpired in their lives. He did not say, "*My great power has made you whole.*" Rather, He said, "*Your faith has made you whole.*"

We see this principle in constant operation throughout the Bible. God responds to faith expressed because it is the currency of heaven. Faith is the key that unlocks the door of blessing within our lives.

What Is Faith?

So, what is faith? In quite simple terms, faith is believing what God said and then declaring it with your own mouth.

> But what does it say? "THE WORD IS NEAR YOU, IN YOUR MOUTH AND IN YOUR HEART" (that is, the word of faith which we preach): that if you confess with your mouth the Lord Jesus and believe in your heart that God has raised Him from the dead, you will be saved. For with the heart one believes unto righteousness, and with the mouth confession is made unto salvation (Romans 10:8-10).

Paul points out that faith is first expressed from your heart in what you believe and then from your mouth in what you say. Both elements are required for faith to be active and alive. So, everything we receive from the Lord is appropriated by faith; there is no other way.

As a part of your covenant, you have already been redeemed from generational curses. Jesus accomplished that at Calvary as part of your salvation. However, it needs to be appropriated by faith in the same way everything else is received. This means I believe and confess that all past generational curses are canceled, null, and void.

Legally Done

Legally, every curse of sin was broken when Jesus' blood was shed. His act of obedience took away every sin that was or ever will be committed. This means that your sin, along with every resulting curse, was nailed to the cross. You and I are now redeemed from the curse that sin produced because of what Jesus accomplished through His substitutionary act at Calvary.

There is no resulting curse or punishment for our sins because Jesus took it upon Himself already.

Just to be clear, this in no way gives us a free ticket to sin. Grace does not give us a license to live according to the dictates of the flesh. It actually empowers us to overcome sin and every unrighteous deed. Paul said it this way, "Shall we continue in sin, that grace may abound? God forbid" (Romans 6:1b-2a, KJV). Freedom from the penalty of sin does not mean that we should live in a careless manner. We have been made free so we can live for Him.

Activating Truth Through Knowledge

In 1993, my wife, Stacey, and I received ministry from a couple by the name of Chester and Betsy Kylstra. It was the first time we had ever heard of the sins of the fathers and resulting curses (we now refer to it as Family DNA). As they ministered to us, we systematically appropriated this element of our redemption of which we had been unaware.

Both of us discovered certain fleshly behaviors that were active within our lives which could be traced back to generational sins and doors that had been opened. These things had transpired in multiple previous generations. As we began to appropriate and receive this element of redemption for our lives, we experienced a new freedom that we did not possess previously. Things that seemed to control our lives ceased to do so any longer.

This all happened because we activated the truth of God's Word by faith. We simply began to receive this element of our redemption, of which we had no previous knowledge. Jesus accomplished it and then gave it to us through the shedding of His blood. However, our ignorance of it caused us to walk in darkness, and thus, we had unknowingly forfeited an element of salvation and deliverance.

> My people are destroyed for lack of knowledge. Because you have rejected knowledge, I also will reject you from being priest for Me; Because you have forgotten the law of your God, I also will forget your children (Hosea 4:6).

Here, we see the root cause for people, even Christians, experiencing destruction in their lives and families. It is a lack of knowledge; it is ignorance. We fail to appropriate the fullness of everything God has provided for us because we lack understanding. It is available, yet our ignorance prevents us from receiving it.

Faith Comes by Hearing

As I said previously, everything that we receive from the Lord is received by faith. However, faith can never move beyond the knowledge of God's Word and His will. This simply means that if we fail to attain knowledge of God's Word, then we will not have faith. Our faith will never be greater than the revealed understanding of God's Word that we possess.

This is the reason that preachers will preach the Word. The knowledge and understanding of God's Word give place for faith to arise, and then we can appropriate God's promise. Paul said, "Faith comes by hearing, and hearing by the word of God" (Romans 10:17). Where there is no hearing of the Word, there is no faith present. Thus, people walk in ignorance and are destroyed for a lack of knowledge; it prevents them from receiving the promises of God.

Although my wife and I had been Christians for our entire lives, we were ignorant of the fact that our family's spiritual DNA was affecting our lives. Therefore, we struggled with certain things needlessly because we merely did not know the root of it. Our ignorance locked us out of this element of our redemption.

The Blessing Is Greater

Please put this to memory: The blessing is greater than the curse! As we reflect on the opening Scripture reference in this chapter, it declares that sin is visited on the third and fourth generation, but obedience causes mercy to be extended to a thousand generations. This means generational blessings are greater than generational curses. Hallelujah!

Jesus destroyed the power of generational curses by becoming a curse as He died on the cross. He did this to cancel every curse and close every open door to the enemy. This means that we can walk free from any penalty of sin, whether it is our own sin or the sins of our fathers. We are free.

Now, as heirs of God, we have been made partakers of His divine nature, and the blessings of the kingdom of God are ours. We live free from any curse brought about through our family DNA because Jesus took it away as He took both the sin and the resulting curse. My friend, this is Good News! You are free!

Family DNA Exercise

Here is a Family DNA Exercise for you to do.

1. Pray and ask the Lord to reveal anything in your family that is a repeating sin pattern or known generational stronghold.

2. Write these things down as God reveals them to you.

3. Declare each one of these things and appropriate the blood of Jesus to blot every one of them out and remove them from your family and generations to come. Declare they are powerless over you because the blood of Jesus is greater!

4. Thank God for your deliverance and freedom from these sinful patterns of past generations and their resulting consequences.

5. Declare and confess that the blessing of Abraham is released in its fullness within your life. Peace, wholeness, and prosperity are your portion. The blessing is greater than the curse!

6

Right Identity by Renewing the Mind

> Do not be conformed to this world, but be transformed by the renewing of your mind (Romans 12:2a).

There are many things that happen to us in life. Our experiences, along with things we hear, cause us to form belief systems. These, in turn, cause us to act and behave in the manner that we do. Our environment trains us about what is good and bad, right and wrong.

All these things begin from the time we are born and can be argued before we take our first breath. Ideas, concepts, and convictions are formed within us, and they drive our personage. Regardless of who or where they come from, it is these things that define our lives as human beings.

A Recreated Spirit

Once someone receives salvation, they are made a new creation in Christ Jesus. Their spirit is recreated, and they become one with the Lord. They become a new species of being in the spirit as their spiritual link to heaven is restored.

This new birth only affects one dimension of our personage, our spirit man. It does not change our soul (mind, will, intellect, and emotions), nor does it change our bodies. The only part of us that changes at the time of salvation is our spirit man.

This means that all the things we believed about the world in which we live, and even the God we serve, did not change at the time of the new birth. Those who previously believed that God desires for them to suffer through life still believe the same thing after the moment of salvation. Our thinking and believing are not automatically changed and transformed when we are born again. Our minds must be renewed.

This is also true concerning our identity, which is what we believe about who we are. This is formed all throughout our time on Earth through both teaching and experience. Mindsets concerning our purpose are determined and set by external components. This means that issues concerning a person's identity remain the same even though they become a child of God. Changes do not happen automatically at the time of salvation.

The Process of Renewing the Mind

When someone experiences the new birth, their spirit is immediately changed. They pass from death to life. They are translated from the kingdom of darkness into the kingdom of God. They go from being bound to being free. It is miraculous and immediate. However, there is a process we must undergo for our minds, thinking, and identity to be changed. Paul called it the renewing of the mind.

We are exhorted not to be conformed to this world but to be transformed. Keep in mind that Paul was speaking to born-again Christians. He said that they were to live in a way that their ideas and behavior did not conform to their environment. He communicated to them that the life experiences which had formed their personage were no longer to be the determining factor within their lives. He exhorted them to be transformed through a process called renewing the mind.

The reality is that throughout our lives, we have been programmed through experiences, education, and family life. However, after we are saved, these things should not continue in the formation of our belief systems. Our thinking and believing must be transformed. We must be changed to think and believe in agreement with God's Word, His will, and His way.

The fact is that the things we have learned through our life experiences are usually not God's way of doing things. What we have been taught or learned about ourselves is usually not what God thinks about us. The world system is not in agreement with the kingdom of God. Therefore, there must be a transformation within our thinking for us to become and identify with all that God has called us to be.

Getting Rid of the Baggage

All of us are brought into the kingdom of God with baggage. Our spirit man is reborn, yet we still possess our old-man thinking and believing. We have many times referred to them as unscriptural or ungodly beliefs. These things are contrary to what God has said in His Word. They are things that we believe about ourselves, others, and the Lord, yet are unscriptural. They are things that do not align with the things that God has spoken clearly within His Word. It is baggage that weighs us down that must be offloaded.

These things may appear to be true, meaning they are experientially correct. However, they are false when measured against God's written Word. They may be accurate in relation to real-life events, yet they fail to align with biblical truths. At this point, we must say, "*Let God be true and every man a liar.*"

Experiences That Form Wrong Thinking

There are various places and experiences from which these types of false beliefs are derived. Childhood hurts and traumas can contribute to these beliefs. Things we experience with fathers, mothers, brothers, sisters, or other family members can all lend themselves to forming these convictions within our minds. These are some of the ways that contribute the most because they involve the people to whom we are closest and have the most influence in our lives.

There are other things that can fortify these types of ungodly beliefs, such as business problems, marital issues, negative church relationships, accidents, tragedies, and natural disasters, to just name a few. All these experiences weigh in on our belief systems. They not only affect what we believe about others but also what we believe about God.

As I shared at the beginning of this book, we experienced a Category 5 hurricane in 2018 named Michael. It was devastating to our region and area, and many people lost their homes and property. For those who looked to pin blame, God became their target. The combination of unbiblical concepts within their minds and then the experience of a devastating storm caused many people to form the conviction that God was the author of the hurricane. This awful storm was sent to teach the people of our region and area some mysterious truth. Their devastating experience caused wrong thinking and believing.

The ungodly belief formed in many people was that God sent calamity and destruction to teach us something. Furthermore, God is the author of everything that happens in the world and has purposed and planned it. People may die in Him conducting His plan, but it is all part of His will and purpose.

Problematic Thinking

The problem with this thinking is that it is unbiblical on numerous levels. **First** and most important, God is good and is always that way. **Second**, everything that happens in the earth is not God's will. Man has a free will and, many times, does not do the will of God. **Thirdly**, storms and natural disasters are the result of the fall of man, not God's providence. Some of it is natural weather patterns that have been in existence for thousands of years, not God sending these things as a means of punishment.

The greatest problem with these ungodly beliefs, besides them being unbiblical, is that they paint a picture in the minds of people that God is the author of destruction. Therefore, whenever something happens that is unexplainable, God is the one who is blamed for it. This is an unbiblical concept that will negatively affect the lives of believers on many different levels.

This type of thinking and believing is problematic and causes numerous issues within the lives of sincere Christians.

The Problematic Cycle

The manner in which ungodly beliefs are developed can vary. However, it usually begins with some sort of experience that turns into a belief, which forms an expectation. That expectation, coupled with confessions and declarations of agreement, will cause fulfillment. It turns into a vicious cycle of experience, belief, expectation, and fulfillment. Then, the cycle continues to repeat itself.

Unfortunately, many well-meaning Christians live on this merry-go-round for their entire existence on Earth. They go round and round with an ever-repeating pattern that God never ordained for them to participate in or experience. It is like a trap that has snared them, and they cannot seem to break free. This is all because of a belief system that has been developed within them. Their experience caused them to believe something untrue, which created expectations that were then fulfilled.

So, this results in never-ending cycles that entrap good people. For this pattern to be disabled, the belief, along with the resulting expectation, must be addressed. Only then can this demonic cycle be destroyed. This is one of the first steps to a permanent life transformation.

Bad Teaching

Another way that these false beliefs are constructed is through unbiblical teaching. Things taught that paint the Heavenly

Father as an angry man just waiting to punish His insolent children result in people having difficulty receiving from the Lord. It produces an unworthiness within the hearts of those who hear and believe these types of incorrect doctrinal instructions concerning the character of God.

Unfortunately, many of us have heard unbiblical things said from the pulpit. This does not mean that our leaders were deceivers; it merely means they were in error. Misunderstanding on the part of the hearer or overemphasis on the part of the teacher has caused everyone to hear things that were not exactly right. Remember, **error always lives right next door to truth.** Any truth that is taken to an extreme or improperly applied will become errant teaching. This will then produce an ungodly belief from which we operate our lives.

The only way to rid yourself of improper beliefs is to replace them with what is correct and balanced. It is not prayed away; it is removed by displacement. We replace what is wrong with what is right. This is the process whereby our minds are renewed with God's Word.

Family Experiences

There can also be improper belief systems developed through family experiences. The things that your parents say to you, whether true or false, affect what you believe about yourself and others. Almost everything we believe about ourselves and the world around us has been influenced by our parents. Usually, what people believe about life in general, politics, education, and the prejudices they may hold were instilled in them by their fathers, mothers, and even grandparents.

Unfortunately, many parents declare things over their children that are contrary to what God says. Things like, "*You will never amount to anything*," or "*You will always not do well in school; your father didn't either*," will cause one to believe things about themself that are not true. These are beliefs that must be deconstructed and changed. These things form strongholds in the mind that dramatically affect personal behavior and accomplishment.

It is amazing how the words of parents and other family members have the power to steer our lives. The ones that we love the most have the greatest influence. We believe what they say because they are our family, and they would certainly tell us nothing but the truth. However, not every word that family members say to us is the truth.

The words spoken to us by our family, along with corresponding experiences, form belief systems within our lives. The words that are not in alignment with God's promises and precepts must be addressed. They must be changed and transformed through the Word of God and the power of the Holy Spirit.

Cultural Influence

Every person born on Earth possesses their own unique experiences that begin the day they are born. These encounters involve the environment they live in, the time during which they exist, and the culture in which they are brought up. The cultural influences of today are different than what they were fifty years ago. Those born in the United States will experience different things from those born in China. Thus, it can be seen how different opinions and convictions may be formed.

All these things that comprise the culture in which we live cause belief systems to be established in our hearts and minds. Things that may be hailed in one nation may be condemned by another. What is exalted in one place can be discouraged in another. The culture we live in determines much of our values and belief systems. Unfortunately, some of these may be unbiblical and false. Yet, they are ingrained within us because we are baptized within a culture where there seems to be no escape.

The only way to address these improper beliefs that poison our hearts and minds is to first identify them by measuring them against the metric of the Bible. If what we believe contradicts Scripture, we have the responsibility to both remove and replace it. This is done through the process of renewing our minds to God's Word.

It Matters What You Believe

You must understand that what you believe matters. What you believe about God, yourself, family members, the church, and your neighbors will affect everything in your life. What you believe about God will determine what you are able to receive from Him. What you believe about yourself will determine what you can accomplish. What you believe about your family will determine the dynamics of your relationships. Every belief influences every realm of your life.

When these beliefs are proper and in alignment with God's promises and precepts, the influence will be positive. However, if these beliefs are incorrect and unbiblical, the influence will be negative. Every biblical belief will produce life, while every ungodly belief will produce destruction.

The bottom line is that failure to address these false belief systems that take root over time will cause us to forfeit many of God's blessings. If we allow these unbiblical beliefs to remain active, they have the potential to damage our relationships, destroy our self-worth, and hinder us from doing the will of God.

Tear It Down

There are many other sources of ungodly and unbiblical beliefs, such as education, unholy alliances, and improper friendships, that we will not take time to discuss fully. However, any belief that we hold that is contrary to what God says in His Word must be torn down. This is one of the keys to seeing healing, deliverance, and restoration in our lives.

> For the weapons of our warfare are not carnal but mighty in God for pulling down strongholds, casting down arguments and every high thing that exalts itself against the knowledge of God, bringing every thought into captivity to the obedience of Christ, (2 Corinthians 10:4-5).

Notice that Paul says that we have been given spiritual weapons of warfare for the purpose of specifically dealing with the things within our thinking and believing—the things within our hearts and minds. He speaks specifically of strongholds, arguments, exalted beliefs contrary to the knowledge of God, and thoughts of disobedience. Paul articulates the need to bring these things into subjection and unseat them from our lives. He speaks specifically of ungodly and unbiblical thinking and believing that keep us in a place of captivity and bondage.

Again, Paul is speaking to Christians who are members of the church at Corinth in this passage of Scripture. He declares that believers have the responsibility of taking up their weapons of spiritual warfare. These strongholds of the mind do not disappear the moment that someone is born again. Salvation is the starting line, not the finish line. Therefore, we must discover our weapons of warfare so that we can deconstruct the ungodly beliefs. Then, we must rebuild the proper structures within our thinking and believing.

The greatest weapon we possess to destroy these strongholds and renew the mind is the truth of God's written Word, the Bible. It is a two-edged sword. One side destroys the old thinking, while the other builds what is proper and correct. It is the sword of the Spirit that can annihilate strongholds within the mind. As this happens, the mind is also renewed and refashioned. This means we have the responsibility of replacing all the stinking thinking of the past with biblical truth.

Metamorphosis

The apostle Paul said we are transformed by the renewing of our minds. The word "transformed" is translated from the Greek word *metamorpho*. It is where we derive our English word "metamorphosis," which is the process by which a caterpillar becomes a butterfly. It spins a cocoon to insulate itself as it undergoes this transformation. Likewise, God's Word becomes the insulating factor within our lives as we undergo a spiritual metamorphosis into who God says we are and what we will be.

We are transformed into His image as we allow His thoughts to become our thoughts. We cease thinking the way the world thinks and begin thinking like Him. The only way for this to happen is to know what He thinks. We discover this through the written Word, the Bible. It gives us insight into His Word, His will, and His ways.

This is a process that requires both time and attention. It will not happen automatically just because you received the gift of salvation. Making Jesus Lord of your life caused your spirit man to be born again, but it did not transform your thinking instantaneously. It is a process that is conducted through the continual application of God's Word within your life.

Dramatic Change

When you consider the metamorphosis whereby a caterpillar becomes a butterfly, it is apparent that the change is dramatic. Butterflies do not look like caterpillars. The worm that once crawled on the ground cannot be compared to the winged creature that floats and flies through the air. The appearance of the two is dramatically different.

In the same way, the transformation that happens within our lives through the renewing of our minds is designed to be just as dramatic. Our lifestyle on the other side of transformation should look dramatically different. Our conduct should not resemble the way our old man behaved. There will be a marked change in the life of the person who has renewed their mind to God's way of thinking and believing.

It is important to understand that without changing the way we think, we will not change the way we believe. If we fail to transform what we believe, we will continue the same life patterns. To see lasting change, we must allow God to bring a metamorphosis in our thinking and believing. That means that we apply ourselves to read and study God's Word. We commit to applying what we learn within our lives. We cast down every thought or imagination that is contrary to what God has declared.

It Is a Process

We live in an "add water and stir" culture. We expect instant results at the snap of our fingers. However, things in the kingdom of God do not operate in that manner. Everything functions by the principle of the seed. This means there is a process of time that is required for maturity to be realized. As the old cliche goes, "***Rome wasn't built in a day.***"

Throughout the Bible, we observe God's Word being likened to seed. There is a lengthy process that is required for a seed to grow to full maturity. It must be planted and watered. There must be warmth for germination to take place. It takes years for an orange seed to become a tree and produce the fruit of oranges.

Jesus said the entire kingdom of God functions in this same manner. This means that spiritual growth, which involves renewing the mind and taking on our true identity, will require a process of time. We grow in grace; we do not leap there. Restoration is an ongoing work of the Holy Spirit within our lives. It is not merely one moment of encounter. Transformation is a process that will continue for our entire lives.

Constant and Continual

There are some improper beliefs that can be changed quickly. Others require a repeated process of continual renewing of the mind. The key to transformation is being constant, steadfast, and faithful throughout this process. Refuse to give up when it seems there is no forward progress. Keep on going when there is adversity and testing. You will come out on the other side with a testimony of victory if you just refuse to quit!

Allow the process to happen within your life. Let God's Word do its work. It will cause your mind to be renewed and your heart to be encouraged. The Word of God will wash and cleanse your mind in the same manner that a shower cleanses your body of earthly contaminants. Let this process begin and then continue in your life. You will see a difference, as will those around you!

Right Identity Exercise

Here are some things to help renew your mind and take on your right identity:

1. Find Scriptures that declare who you are in Christ—those verses that say "*in Him.*" This is who you really are.

2. Put these verses to memory and say them every day.

3. Choose to believe what God says about you.

4. List things that are contrary to what the Bible says that you have believed about yourself—identify it and commit to never again speaking it about yourself.

5. Find at least one Scripture to replace and counteract your previous identities—say them daily.

7
Your Words Have Power

> You are snared by the words of your mouth;
> You are taken by the words of your mouth (Proverbs 6:2).

Many years ago, a gentleman came in for counseling regarding issues going on in his life. There was a myriad of things taking place that were plaguing him. He was having difficulty in his family, finances, and career.

As he began to share his predicament, I noticed that he was quite negative about all the things he had encountered. As I dug a little deeper, I realized that some things he said were exaggerations and overstatements of reality. There were things genuinely wrong, but less than what he portrayed.

One of the first things I asked him concerned his family. It became apparent that his normal conversation with his wife revolved around the problems they were having and his daily critique of her. So, I asked him, "*Do you tell your wife every day that you love her and that she is beautiful? Do you tell her how much you appreciate her and how life would not be the same without her? Do you tell her what a wonderful job she does and how she helps make your house a home?*" He looked puzzled for a moment and then replied, "*Well,... no!*"

He continued by saying, "*We just typically talk about our financial situation and how it seems she's spending all the money.*" I then asked him how that was working out. He said, "*It's not.*" I then asked him, "*Are things any better since you've been having these discussions?*" He said, "*No, they are actually getting worse.*" I then told him that he needed to take a different approach.

The Need for Change

From there I proceeded to explain to him the necessity of changing his conversation. I explained that his words were empowering the undesirable. As the man of the house, he was unknowingly using his tongue as an agent of cursing. I encouraged him to wake up every morning and speak words of affirmation to his wife. I also told him to stop having these discussions that focused on the challenges they were facing. Instead, I instructed him to change the conversation by talking about what they desired to enjoy in their future, along with God's promise to see it happen.

He went home and started doing what I advised. Over the course of time, things revolutionized in his life. Things began moving in a new direction. There was a breakthrough in their marriage and finances. He had a new outlook on life and started smiling. God revolutionized this man's life when he changed his conversation. When he began speaking life rather than death, God restored his marriage and family.

> But no man can tame the tongue. It is an unruly evil, full of deadly poison. With it we bless our God and Father, and with it we curse men, who have been made in the similitude of God. Out of the same mouth proceed blessing and cursing. My brethren, these things ought not to be so (James 3:8-10).

The apostle James exhorted believers to refrain from speaking things that are contrary to the heart of God. There is a biblical admonition to guard the words that come out of our mouths. This is something that is declared in both the Old and New Testaments of the Bible. It is a kingdom principle that must be acknowledged and embraced by all believers who desire to walk in freedom and experience complete restoration.

We Must Harness Our Words

There are many believers who fail to walk in the abundant life that Jesus promised solely because they have neglected to harness the words of their mouths. They say things that are unbiblical and untrue. These words uttered become an open door for the enemy to take advantage of them. They are snared with the very words of their mouth.

These same believers will then question the predicaments in which they find themselves. They will scratch their heads in bewilderment and wonder why the blessing of the Lord has somehow escaped them. They need to look no further than the thing that is in their mouth. Their tongue has given an opportunity for the curse to be empowered and wreak havoc.

The Untamed Tongue is Poisonous

James said that the tongue was full of deadly poison, speaking specifically of the untamed tongue. The person who fails to tame their tongue and bring it into subjection to the Holy Spirit has a deadly weapon inside their mouth. Think about that! Unfortunately, an untamed tongue releases its deadly poison and affects the person doing the speaking more than anyone else. It harms the body in which it is housed. It becomes a self-destruct mechanism when it is not harnessed.

Here is the unfortunate truth: Most believers are unaware that they are harming themselves by the words of negativity that they speak. They snare themselves with the words that are coming out of their mouths.

Sometimes, these things are said in the name of being humble. They can even be said in a manner of self-deprecation. However, the effect may still be the same. It damages and hurts the individual who is speaking. Their tongue becomes like the fangs of a deadly rattlesnake that poisons its victims. The unfortunate thing is that those who fail to harness their tongue victimize themselves. The devil is nowhere in sight. They hurt themselves.

The Command of Harnessing the Tongue

As Christians, we must understand that it is a command for us to refrain from speaking words that embody doubt, unbelief, negativity, hatred, malice, envy, and many other things that are contrary to the nature of God. This is not something that is optional for believers. God commanded it!

James specifically said that we should not bless God but then curse men (which includes ourselves). Let me break this down for you. He said that we were not to come to church, praise and worship the Lord, shout, dance, and rejoice in the presence of God, but then leave the church and talk bad about our brothers and sisters in Christ. James said that these things should not be taking place.

Unfortunately, this type of behavior happens far too often in the body of Christ. People will lift their hands and praise God all over the church building. Then, they will go home and have fried deacon, roasted worship leader, and char-broiled pastor for Sunday dinner. It is duplicitous for anyone to do this, and the Bible frowns on it. If you have done it before, ask for forgiveness. If you still do it, then add stop to that equation.

Here is the truth: You will never experience God's restorative power if you cannot harness your tongue. Words of negativity will function as a stricture and then block the flow of God's blessings. Put this simple truth to memory, and it will save you a lot of trouble. **Words of cursing stop the flow of blessing.**

> A man's stomach shall be satisfied from the fruit of his mouth; From the produce of his lips, he shall be filled. Death and life are in the power of the tongue, And those who love it will eat its fruit (Proverbs 18:20-21).

Notice these verses of Scripture communicate that the words you speak have power, and your life will be filled with things that align with what you say. It declares that the fruit we reap within our lives has a direct correlation to the words coming out of our mouths.

Our Words Have Power

The things we speak about ourselves have more power within our lives than anything that anyone else could ever say about us. Most people find themselves where they are today because of things they said yesterday. It is not what others have said about them. Those words have no power unless someone believes and receives them.

Many people release curses by saying things that are contrary to the promises of God. When believers do this, it creates a blockade that prevents God's promise from being fulfilled. It is like spraying weed killer on a rose bloom. It kills the bloom and goes all the way down into the root.

One translation of the previous verse of Scripture is that *those who show attention to what they say will love its fruit*. It is important to watch what you say. Thoughts that come through your brain do not necessitate being spoken. Truthfully, most of them should not be said. If it is not wholesome, then it should not proceed from your mouth. If it is not godly, then remain quiet.

Your Words Are Seeds for Your Future

The Bible declares the wholesome tongue is a tree of life. Again, we continually see how the tongue is compared to seeds, plants, trees, and fruit. It reveals that the words we speak are seeds that eventually grow and produce a harvest within our lives. Your words are the seeds that are planted for the future you will experience. This is an irrefutable kingdom principle that cannot be changed. God is the one who instituted this eternal law.

Your words have the power to produce. What you say will determine what is created and then grows in your life. You decide what is planted and produced by the words of your mouth. If you desire to see the promise of God grow and manifest, then speak it out. Let it become the declaration spoken over your life. The more you say these things, the more the seed is watered and grows.

We must take a close examination of the words we speak. Be honest with yourself and closely examine what you say about yourself and others on a regular basis. Are you articulating words of life and restoration or death and tragedy? Are you regularly speaking about healing and well-being or sickness and pain? Are you consistently declaring victory, or is it the drone of defeat?

The Tongue Is Like a Rudder

You are going to experience the very things to which you give power with the words of your mouth. The tongue is what gives these things the ability to live and abide in your life. It is the words of your mouth that set the course for your life, like a rudder on a ship. The apostle James said this:

> Indeed, we put bits in horses' mouths that they may obey us, and we turn their whole body. Look also at ships: although they are so large and are driven by fierce winds, they are turned by a very small rudder wherever the pilot desires. Even so the tongue is a little member and boasts great things. See how great a forest a little fire kindles! (James 3:3-5).

The tongue is compared to the rudder on a ship. James declares that the tongue steers your life. It is not the words that others speak or say but rather what proceeds from your mouth. This is what has power in your life. The opinions of others have far less power over you than the words you speak about your own existence.

The amazing thing about a rudder on a sailing vessel is that even when contrary winds are blowing, the ship can still be steered in the right direction. James is declaring that the storms of life can be overcome if you turn the rudder in the right direction. It is turned by your words.

The issue that many believers have is that when winds of adversity blow, they allow the wind to control their rudders. They steer their vessel in the same direction as the wind. So, if a gust of financial lack is blowing, they talk about the lack rather than the promise of provision. If the storm of marital discord arrives, they talk about their spouse's issues rather than rehearsing the wonderful things God has done in their marriage. Unfortunately, they steer with the wind and are overcome by it when all they need to do is use their rudder to send their vessel in the right direction. Think about that for a moment!

Regardless of the Wind, The Tongue Steers

So often, we point the finger and blame people and circumstances for our unpleasantries. Many times, we blame the devil for the adversity that we encounter. I understand that people, uncontrollable circumstances, and the devil can all play a part in creating negative experiences within our lives.

However, the point that James makes is that with the tongue, your ship can be steered in the right direction and weather the storm. Regardless of what people do or say, you can come through it with a testimony of victory. The devil has no authority in your life, so you can overcome and triumph despite the attack. Glory to God!

The key to all of this is the declaration of the promise of God in the middle of every circumstance. Refuse to allow words of doubt, unbelief, and negativity to proceed out of your mouth. Instead, speak life, healing, and breakthrough. Declare what God has said about you throughout His Word. This is the way that you navigate through the storm and come out unscathed.

You are the one who sets the course of your life. You do it with the words that you speak. Your tongue steers the ship of your life. What you say will determine your destination and place of arrival. Where do you want to go? Where do desire to arrive? Let the Word of God be your GPS and follow the path that it sets by speaking His promises!

Your Tongue Determines Your Outcome

The writer of Proverbs said, "Death and life are in the power of the tongue" (Proverbs 18:21). So, we see that the tongue can release death or life. You make the determination of what will reign in your family and personage. Your outcome is controlled by the thing that resides inside your mouth, the tongue.

I have heard people say that God led them down certain roads, which ended in tragedy. They desired to blame God for their situation and what happened. They did not want to take any responsibility for their outcome. The truth is that their tongue did the steering along with their own decision-making and actions.

God gave man free will to make decisions and choices. Right decisions and choices will produce life and blessings. Wrong decisions and choices will produce heartache and destruction. It is just that simple. The things you choose and allow to proceed out of your mouth will produce your eventual outcome. There is no predestination that God forces on us outside of the choices that we make. The will of God is only fulfilled when we speak right and make correct decisions. That is what steers our life.

Jesus Takes the Wheel with Your Tongue

Many years ago, there was a popular song that was released entitled "Jesus, Take The Wheel." There are many people who believe that if they just sing the song or say the title, God will be in control of their lives. However, God is only in control of our lives to the degree that we speak in agreement with His will and purpose. God cannot be in control when our tongue is yielded to the words of the enemy—words of doubt, unbelief, sin, hatred, and malice. Jesus takes the wheel when our tongue is aligned with His Word!

Some believers think that if they pray for God to take control of their lives that somehow everything they do and experience will be God-ordained. Unfortunately, this is not the truth. While it is a good thing to verbally submit yourself to the Lord on a regular basis, if you do not harness your tongue and speak the right things, God has no ability to change the course of your life.

This truth in no way diminishes the power of God working within you. It is just the realization that God cannot work His will if we speak things that are contrary to it. We are steering in the opposite direction of Him when we say things that are contrary to His promises and covenant. Therefore, we tie the hands of the Lord to work His plan that He desires for us.

For us to experience the fullness of God's restorative power, we must align our conversation with His promise. On the heels of Hurricane Michael, when people were saying that our city and region would die, we chose to speak God's promise. We declared that He would restore, and it would be better than before. *Jehovah-SHALAM* arose, and His Word triumphed. It happened because we spoke what we believed rather than what we saw at the moment.

There were reports saying that the Air Force base in our area would be permanently shut down. We chose to believe and say something different. We declared that we would have more than we had before! We steered our ship with the rudder we were given, our tongue. The base was not dismantled; rather, it was rebuilt. Now it is referred to as the military base of the future. Glory to God!

The Rudder Is Greater than the Wind

Even when winds blow (and they will), your tongue can keep your ship going in the right direction. In adverse conditions, you hold your course by continuing to speak and declare the promise of God. When you echo what God said, the words of your mouth are more powerful than the contrary winds that blow. Do not believe that you are helpless and cannot do anything to improve your situation. Rise up and shout what God has declared. Stand out on the bow of your ship and say, "*Peace, be still!*"

One of the things that James points out is that even though the rudder is small, it will take the vessel wherever the pilot desires. The rudder, which is your tongue, will steer you to wherever you want to go. This is the reason we must speak where we want to go rather than what we see at the moment.

Perhaps you desire to see a strong and thriving marriage rather than the one you see that is failing. Start speaking life over your relationship. Let the rudder, although it may be small, steer your marriage to a place of restoration. Even though you may be in the storm, direct it to a harbor of safety with the words that are coming from your mouth. This is the way you arrive at the place that you desire.

Doors Are Opened Through Words

It is important to realize that even though a Christian is redeemed from the curse (Galatians 3:13), it can still be empowered and released within their lives by the words of their mouth. If we speak words that agree with the curse, we will open the door for it to enter our lives. Words released out of your mouth that agree with the lie of the enemy will produce the undesirable. Even though we have been purchased by the blood of Jesus and the curse of hell has no right to any area of our life, the words we speak can empower the will of satan if what we speak is contrary to God's promise.

James said that out of the same mouth proceeds blessing and cursing. He went on to say that this should not be taking place. In other words, do not allow words that release the curse to come out of your mouth. Choose to speak life and restoration. Declare the promises of God and allow His blessing to overflow.

My father taught me growing up that if I could not say something good, then say nothing at all. That is a good motto for all of us to live by. If you cannot say things that bless and edify both you and those around you, then choose to remain silent. Let your mouth be a well of life and blessing. Let it minister grace to everyone who hears you.

> In the beginning God created the heavens and the earth. The earth was without form, and void; and darkness was on the face of the deep. And the Spirit of God was hovering over the face of the waters. Then God said, "Let there be light"; and there was light (Genesis 1:1-3).

At the dawn of creation, God demonstrates this kingdom principle. It is found in the first three verses of Scripture within our Bible. God stepped out into the middle of darkness and said, "*Let there be light.*"

It is important for us to consider what God did not say. He did not make commentary on the darkness. He did not say, "*Wow, it sure is dark out here!*" No, God spoke "light" in the middle of darkness. When He was surrounded by a great abyss of void and dark, He declared light!

God demonstrated the necessity to speak what you desire, not what you see. He revealed the importance of declaring light and life when you are surrounded by darkness and destruction. God displayed that speaking the right thing changes the wrong thing.

Words Create Your World

The account of creation that we read in our Bible is not merely to reveal God's great power. It is there for us to observe kingdom principles in action so we can experience the same thing. Those things are written so we can imitate God and experience the miraculous in our lives. If you find yourself surrounded by darkness, begin to speak light rather than discuss how dark it may be. If you are in a situation of oppression, then speak freedom and deliverance.

Your words have the power to create the world in which you live. Many times, people blame the devil for what they have created for themselves. The problem was that they were saying the wrong things. Instead of creating a world of blessing, they created one of pain and heartache because of what they continually spoke.

You can create a different atmosphere for you and your family. You can create a good atmosphere wherever you find yourself. You do it with the words you speak. Declaring God's Word and promises will foster an atmosphere of life. This can be applied in any area of your life, whether it be marriage, family, health, finances, or emotional well-being. You must ask yourself what you desire to see in manifestation. Then, speak the promises of God that assure you of these things.

> A man has joy by the answer of his mouth,
> And a word spoken in due season, how good it is! (Proverbs 15:24).

I am sure that all of us know people who never have anything good to say. They are like a spiritual Eeyore, like the donkey character in ***Winnie the Pooh***. They live on the dark side of life. Nothing is ever right. They seem to find the cloud in the silver lining rather than the other way around. They say things that are depressive and are the rain on a sunny day. Unfortunately, the more someone speaks in this manner, the worse things will become. They curse their own existence with words of negativity.

Hee-Haw

I remember when I was a young boy, there was television series that aired on the weekend called ***Hee-Haw***. It was a country music comedy show that had a barnyard setting. There were jokes and comedic skits that were performed with piped-in laughs.

There was one skit that was performed every show, featuring four men dressed in overalls—a quartet. They would all sing this song where each individual would sing a line expressing their sadness and depression. The chorus of the song contained these lyrics:

> Gloom, despair, and agony on me.
> Deep dark depression, excessive misery
> If it weren't for bad luck, I'd have no luck at all.
> Gloom, despair, and agony on me!

The song was comedic in nature, and everyone laughed. However, this is the way that many people live their lives. They sing the sad songs of their existence to everyone they are around, even when they are by themselves. Things are constantly bad and getting worse. They become the antidote for joy and happiness. They are snared with the words of their own mouths.

Things Can Change

However, this can all be changed. Joy can be released in your life just by the words that you speak. Your disposition can be turned around based on what you talk about. Like King David at Ziklag, you can encourage yourself in the Lord even when you experience loss. It is a choice that you make. You can choose depression, or you can choose joy. You can choose death, or you can choose life. Joy and life are much better!

The apostle Paul said that the kingdom of God is righteousness, peace, and joy in the Holy Ghost. He did not say it is sin, turmoil, and depression from hell. To see the kingdom manifested in your life, you must begin to speak things that are joyful and edifying. Confessing and declaring the promises of God will bring joy to your heart and restoration to your soul. It will stir up the good things of God and bring them into a place of manifestation.

We have all heard the old saying, "*The pen is mightier than the sword.*" Let me break this down for you: Words are stronger and have greater influence than physical power and might. We often think that we could fix things if we had more authority, power, or money. If we possessed all the necessary natural things, then we could see a turnaround.

The truth is you already have what you need. It is in your mouth. When you start speaking things in alignment with God's Word, things will begin to transform. They may not change immediately. However, over the course of time, as you continue to release the Word of the Lord from your mouth, you will see your desire fulfilled.

Words Will Stir Up

For those of us who are married, we recognize how saying the wrong things can bring about unpleasant responses from our spouse. I recall many years ago, not long after my wife, Stacey, and I were married, we were getting ready for a Sunday morning church service. We were running a little late, and I was a bit frustrated. My wife asked me, "*How do I look?*" I abruptly responded, "*Fine!*"

Unfortunately, the way I responded communicated that I did not care how she looked. We were running behind and needed to leave immediately. This resulted in taking another 15 minutes of precious time as she proceeded to change her clothing.

The words that I spoke released something in the atmosphere of my home. Instead of love, care, and approval, I released careless feelings, frustration, and impatience. In this situation, it was not the word I used, but the intent of my heart in how I said it.

So, the principle we see is that words can stir up things, good or bad. If you are believing God for the restoration of your marriage, then speak words that will stir up love and appreciation. Refuse to say things that will harm the restoration process. Saying the wrong things is working against God. We co-labor with the Lord when we say the things that He has spoken in His Word.

Encouraging Words

Everyone needs to be encouraged. It does not matter who you are, where you live, or how much money you have in the bank. Every person desires to hear something good spoken to and about them. The greatest way to encourage others and be encouraged is with words of reassurance and affirmation. As I alluded to earlier, the Bible declares that David encouraged himself in the Lord.

> And David was greatly distressed; for the people spoke of stoning him, because the soul of all the people was grieved, every man for his sons and for his daughters: but David encouraged himself in the LORD his God (1 Samuel 30:6).

When you read the full account of everything that took place in this story, we observe David assisting another king in dealing with a common enemy, the Philistines. David left his family and all their possessions in a city called Ziklag. After returning from the battle, they discovered that the Amalekites had invaded the city and burned it down. To make matters worse, their families had been kidnapped, and all their possessions had been stolen.

At the sight of the devastation, David and his men were so saddened that they wept until they had no more strength to weep. It was so bad that the men who had loyally followed

David spoke of stoning him. I am not sure that David would have objected since the pain he felt was so deep at that moment. However, the tide turned when David chose to use his rudder to change the direction that the ship was sailing. He encouraged himself in the Lord.

The Word of "*SHALAM*"

David began to seek the Lord and worship Him. He put on the priestly garment that was worn for worship and the offering of sacrifices. He began to offer the sacrifice of praise—the fruit of his lips giving thanks to the name of the Lord. As he did, the Lord spoke prophetically for David to pursue, overtake, and recover all. Let me say it another way, "*SHALAM!*"

God assured him that everything would be restored. The word of the Lord comforted and encouraged David. So, they pursued the enemy, overtook them, and recovered all that had been stolen.

> And David recovered all that the Amalekites had carried away: and David rescued his two wives. And there was nothing lacking to them, neither small nor great, neither sons nor daughters, neither spoil, nor any thing that they had taken to them: David recovered all. And David took all the flocks and the herds, which they drave before those other cattle, and said, This is David's spoil (1 Samuel 30:18-20, KJV).

Not only did David get back everything that was stolen, but also the spoils of the battle. He ended up with MORE THAN

HE HAD BEFORE! God brought restoration of all that had been stolen. If He did it for David, He will do it for you!

Use Your Rudder to Overcome

David faced a fork in the road when he returned to Ziklag. It would have been easy for him to succumb to the voice of emotions. He could have easily had a pity party and remained there. He had the opportunity to sing a song like the "Hee-Haw" song of gloom and despair. Unfortunately, he would have died in doing so. Instead, David chose to encourage himself in the Lord; he worshipped God and sought the word of the Lord. He used the rudder on his ship to sail into the wind of adversity and experienced a mighty breakthrough and restoration. David's words were the catalyst to release the power to overcome.

When you are faced with negative situations, speak restoration and deliverance. If you encounter the winds of hardship or difficulty, do not panic. Take hold of your rudder and declare that you will overcome. Being more than a conqueror in Christ does not guarantee the absence of adversity, but it does assure us that we will triumph in the end. However, **we must speak the end from the beginning**. We don't wait until the battle is over; we shout now! We shout victory when things are in a place of defeat. We shout healing when sickness is raging. Why do we do that? It is because that is how the rudder of your tongue will steer you out of the situation.

> He sent His word and healed them, And delivered them from their destructions (Psalm 107:20).

We must understand that our words have the power to hurt or to heal—to bind the wound or pour salt into it. We see that God heals through the Word that He speaks. Likewise, we can bring healing and deliverance if we will choose to speak what God says instead of the chaos we witness around us.

Choose Your Words Wisely

We must choose our words wisely and only speak things that align with God's promises. Make a choice today to speak life and restoration. Choose to declare healing, wholeness, and deliverance. Speak God's promises that He has declared over your life. Every promise in the Bible belongs to you, so believe it and receive it. This is the pathway to restoration.

The words you speak will be like the rudder that guides your ship into the port of restoration. *Jehovah-SHALAM* will arise, and you will see every promise fulfilled within your life. It belongs to you; now seize it in Jesus' name!

Aligning Your Words Exercise

Here are some things you can do to align your words with God's promises and declarations.

1. Pray and ask God to reveal any place where your words have been sabotaging your life and family.

2. Write down anything God reveals that you should change in your conversation.

3. Replace any words of negativity with a promise found in God's Word, the Bible.

4. Daily, speak aloud the promises and declarations that God has impressed on your heart.

5. Thank God daily for freedom and restoration, that you will recover all that has been stolen.

8

Healing Is the Children's Bread

> Who Himself bore our sins in His own body on the tree, that we, having died to sins, might live for righteousness—by whose stripes you were healed. For you were like sheep going astray, but have now returned to the Shepherd and Overseer of your souls (1 Peter 2:24-25).

I recognize that every person on this planet has experienced hurt in their lives. The reality is that it starts at birth. Most children are born in a manner that squeezes them as they traverse through a narrow passage. They travel from a place of total darkness into lights that are shining with the brightness of the Sun. They move from an environment that is warm and comfortable into an operating room that is just above the temperature needed to store meat. It is like getting out of a hot tub outside on a freezing day in Alaska.

As soon as a baby is delivered, nurses will take the newborn and lay it on a table. Granted, it is warmer, but it is sterile and stiff, unlike the environment that the baby came from, which was safe and squishy. They are scrubbed with towels that feel like sandpaper and then given shots. If that is not enough, they put ointment in their eyes that burns and causes swelling. This is a child's first experience. Welcome to Earth!

Living in a Fallen World

The reality is that living in a fallen world means that all of us will have undesirable experiences. Things happen to us physically, emotionally, and spiritually. Some are good, and some are bad. Some bring pleasure, and some bring pain. We witness the blessing and the curse existing together in a world that has fallen from grace.

The unfortunate reality is that while traversing down the road of life, hurt is inevitable. It is an unpleasant fact. It does not matter if you are a good or bad person, saved or unsaved. Pain is something that we all will encounter on our journey. None of us can totally escape the challenges that are brought by living on this wonderful planet called Earth. Along with the rose, comes the thorns.

The Experiences of Life

Life's experiences bring us much joy, but unfortunately, some of them bring us pain. It is not merely physical pain, but emotional also. As we travel through life, things happen to us that inflict blows on our human psyche, which often cause a distortion of our perspective. We then peer at life through the lens of the pain and hurt we experienced. We see others through the harm that we have emotionally felt.

Sometimes, similar events transport us back to the moment of the original hurt. We relive the event repeatedly anytime something happens to us that resembles the experience that caused the pain. The only way that this roller coaster stops is to be emotionally and mentally healed.

Jesus took stripes upon His back for our healing. He paid the price for you to experience and walk in spiritual, physical, mental, and emotional health. The same stripes he took for your physical healing also provided emotional healing. No stone was left unturned, and God's covenant of healing can be received for every area of your life. He is *Jehovah-Rapha*, the Lord your healer.

It is More than "Get Over It!"

In the past, many have understated the reality of emotional hurt and the need for emotional healing. Some would say, "*They just need to get over it.*" I agree that sometimes people hold on to petty things that can easily be overcome; they make mountains out of molehills. However, things that cut to the core of someone's emotional personage are much more difficult to overcome. No one should ever diminish the pain someone experienced solely because it was not physical in nature.

We must realize that there is a process required for people to "get over it." One cannot just flip the "get over it" switch and suddenly all the pain disappears. Your human psyche does not operate in that manner. It is like someone who breaks their arm; there is no "get over it" button that can be pushed that resets the bone and causes it to be instantaneously healed.

We would never even dream of telling someone who has a physical ailment to just "get over it." However, we do not seem to have the same apprehension when it comes to emotional or mental ailments. Some of this happened in the past because of ignorance related to emotional illness. Today, there is a much greater understanding that should promote a new level of compassion toward those who suffer in these arenas.

Ouch! My Eye

Many years ago, our family visited Orlando to go to Disney World®. We stayed in a beautiful hotel near the Magic Kingdom and proceeded to prepare for a day in the park. Our oldest son and daughter-in-law, Joshua and Miranda, were with us, and we all expected a fun-filled day together.

Before we left the hotel, my wife and I visited the room where my son and his family were staying. Our grandson, Josiah, was sitting up in bed and smiling. So, I decided to play Peek-a-boo with him while using my wife as my shield. I would peer out from behind her and say, "Peek-a-boo," and he would laugh. Everything was wonderful, and we were having a blast.

While I was doing this, my wife, Stacey, reached up with the intention of patting me on my face. She was attempting to be affectionate and let me know that she loved me. Unfortunately, she missed my face, and her fingernail went straight into my eye. All the laughter suddenly stopped as I shouted out in pain. It was one of the most excruciating events that I had ever experienced.

I immediately went to the sink in the bathroom because it felt as though there was a stick in my eye. I attempted to wash it thoroughly, thinking that once this object in my eye was rinsed away, the pain would be relieved. Unfortunately, regardless of the amount of flushing, the pain never subsided.

Suck it Up and Keep Going

I thought to myself that it would eventually stop hurting. So, we proceeded with our day. I had always been taught to just "suck it up" and keep on going. So, that is what I did. Our first stop was the Disney Springs® (formerly Downtown Disney®) area, where we walked around and visited different retail outlets that were open. The pain was not subsiding, and if anything, it was getting worse.

We eventually decided to eat at a restaurant called T-Rex®. In this eating establishment, there are various dining areas where lights flash throughout your dining experience, along with the sounds of roaring dinosaurs and some animatronics. I could hardly eat because my eye was hurting so badly. I began to feel nauseated by the pain combined with the overstimulation of the lights and sound.

At the end of the meal, I attempted to walk around for a moment, but the pain continued, and it would not subside. I was hoping that it would go away so we could enjoy the day, but it only persisted. I finally told my wife, "*We need to leave and return home.*" We cut our trip short because I could not bear the pain any longer, combined with the nausea it was generating. So, we told our son and his family we were going home, kissed our grandson on the head, and off we went.

Going Home

Since I normally drove, I got in the driver's seat of our SUV and began the six-hour journey. My wife knew that the pain I was experiencing had to be extreme, when thirty minutes down the road, I asked her to drive. I told her I could not drive any longer, and the only way I could feel any semblance of relief was to close my eyes. So, for the remaining portion of the trip, she drove while I would cry out in pain and stomp my feet on the floorboard from time to time. In all our married life, she had never seen me do anything like this; it was out of character for me. My wife knew that I was not exaggerating and that the pain was real. As we were driving, she repeatedly apologized for what had happened, even though it was not done intentionally. It was purely accidental. However, the apology did not take the pain away.

Fortunately, one of our founding church members, Paul McGoey, was an optometric assistant. My wife called him while we were driving and set up an emergency appointment. We drove straight to their office, where both the doctor and his nurse were waiting for me since we arrived after their normal hours.

The Doctor Visit

As soon as we arrived, I walked into the office, and they put me in an examination chair. The nurse applied what I referred to as "magic drops" in my eye. Every bit of pain instantly stopped. This was the first time in my life that I wanted to kiss a nurse. It was amazing; all the displeasure was gone. Praise the Lord!

The doctor came in to examine my eye. I told him what happened and how my injury took place. After looking at it, he announced to me and my wife:

> "Well, she did it good. She tore four layers of your cornea, which has only five layers. I've had

> big bodybuilders come in here with similar injuries crawling on their knees. There are more nerve endings in this part of your eye than in any other part of your body. You experienced a code 4 alarm when it happened."

I cannot tell you how vindicated I felt at that moment. My pain was validated and could be understood. Just knowing that what I was feeling was justifiable made me feel better about everything.

The Prescription

Then, the doctor placed a patch on my eye. It amounted to a clear contact lens coated with an anti-bacterial ointment. He told me to leave it on for three days. I immediately noticed that I could not see clearly—everything was blurred. The doctor also told me that I would not be able to drive for a couple of weeks while my eye healed. He told me that after the contact was removed, I was to keep ointment on it for several weeks and especially at night to prevent the underside of my eyelid from sticking to the wound on my eye. If that happened, it would injure my eye again.

So, for the next several weeks, I could not see clearly. The injury I experienced affected my eyesight while it was in the healing process. Eventually, my eye healed, and all was fine. My vision returned to normal, and I have never had any problem since then.

There are so many principles and truths that can be derived from this personal story. It reveals how personal injuries happen while living in this world. Many of them are accidental—not intentional. The pain remains until it is addressed. There is a healing process for things to be restored and return to normal. Many times, we cannot see properly because of the hurt while it heals. You may have to get someone else to guide you and help you navigate through the situation when pain is present. We will speak in more detail about each one of these things mentioned.

Emotional Pain is Real

It is important to understand that emotional pain is just as real as physical pain. Many times, the hurt someone experiences emotionally can scream louder and be more excruciating than physical pain. The process for emotional healing is much like physical healing. It does not happen overnight; there is time involved for restoration to take place. We cannot snap our fingers and have everything restored.

Even when Jesus ministered to people, many of them were healed as they went their way. There was a process. Likewise, there is time involved in the manifestation of emotional healing.

Most emotional hurt that people experience is not the result of someone intentionally attempting to inflict pain. The bulk of things that happen are more accidental in nature. Much of it comes from the people we love the most and who love us the most. It is much more difficult to experience emotional damage from someone you do not know from Adam's house cat. It is the people that we hold dear who have the greatest potential of hurting us emotionally.

Pain Caused by People Close to You

When I experienced my eye injury, it happened because I was close to my wife at that moment. Think about that; it was because I was near her. It was not done intentionally, but it still caused me great pain. We must understand that people who are close to us do not usually intentionally do things to harm us. Things just happen in life while existing in this fallen world. Many times, people say and do things unknowingly that administer pain to our emotions. Our feelings are hurt because of something we perceive as a personal offense or attack, whether it was or not.

When these types of things happen, the normal human response is to retaliate or demand the individual repair what was harmed through an apology and confession of their wrong. However, even when these things are done, it does not necessarily repair the damage. My wife was sincerely apologetic for the injury to my eye. However, it did not cause the pain to go away. Neither will an apology alone bring healing to an emotional injury. Only God's Word and His power can bring healing and restoration.

Forgive and Release for Healing to Begin

One of the steps to receiving healing is to forgive and release those who harmed us. We cannot hold others responsible for the rest of our lives due to the hurt that was administered. We cannot expect them to repay us for all that we suffered at their hand. My friend, at the end of the day, this disposition is a dead-end street. It will only foster bitterness and resentment. Even if they do their best to return what you believe was stolen or taken away, the pain will still be there until you allow Jesus to minister to you and bring restoration. He is the only one who can restore you.

I recognize that there are times when people do things intentionally to cause pain. They intend on doing something to render some type of wound to an individual. Regardless of their intent, the response is still the same for us to be healed and walk in freedom. We must forgive, let go of the hurt and offense, and allow God to heal us.

How often have you heard someone say, "*Well, they haven't apologized, so I'm not forgiving them until they do?*" I have heard people say this. The reality is that until they choose to forgive, their pain will continue. The act of issuing an apology will not remove the hurt, but the act of forgiving will start the process. We must articulate forgiveness even if someone never apologizes. Doing what is right should not be predicated on someone's admission of their wrong. Choose to forgive regardless of their issuance of an apology.

Forgiveness Is not Optional

In a previous chapter, I wrote in detail about forgiveness. Jesus commanded us to forgive; it is not optional for Christians. One of the greatest obstacles people face in extending forgiveness is that the hurt they feel shouts at them. The pain prevents them from forgiving because the emotions that are present can be extremely difficult to overcome. All of us have been at this place at some moment in our lives. However, the healing we need cannot begin until we embark on the journey of forgiveness. It is the prerequisite.

Forgiving others is a deliberate act just like receiving your emotional healing. Neither happens automatically, and time alone cannot bring the healing and restoration you need. Taking action to forgive and receive your healing is the key to having your emotional well-being restored. Holding on to the hurt will not produce good fruit. Stuffing it will only lead to emotional infection. Things will fester like a diseased sore, which will eventually cause even worse problems within one's life.

Obtaining Help

There are times when it is necessary to get someone to help you navigate through emotional hurt. When my eye was injured, I could not drive. I had to depend on my wife to transport me since I could not see clearly.

When someone is hurt emotionally, the pain of the moment can many times be blinding, to the point that they cannot see the road they need to travel. It is good to have someone that you can confide in who will speak the truth to you. You do not need someone who will take your offense, villainize your offender, and then wish your common enemy some type of harm. Someone giving you pity and cheering you on to despise and be bitter at another person is not what is needed.

The reality is that when we are hurt, we cannot see clearly. Everything looks distorted and fuzzy. When someone is hurt, even a kind word can be heard as criticism. When someone is carrying around emotional pain, a slap on the back from someone complimenting them may be received as a verbal attack. The bottom line is that **hurt people cannot perceive correctly**.

We Need Truth Spoken to Us

Everyone needs at least one person who will tell them the truth and give sound advice. That counsel begins with, "*You must forgive and receive healing!*" I recognize this is not what anyone wants to hear when they have been harmed. Our fallen human nature, combined with an unrenewed mind, will shout for vindication. However, that will not bring healing or restoration. It will only make things worse.

I have found that many people will shout about knowing the truth, but fewer are as excited when it shows up. The truth may not be what we always want to hear, and it will challenge us most of the time. However, the truth is what will set us free and bring healing to our spirit, soul, and body.

Sometimes you may need someone to hold your hand and walk with you through the healing process. That does not mean that you are a weak individual. It means that you are hurt and in need of help. Who has not been in a similar situation at some point in their life? We have all been there. There is no shame in getting someone to minister to you and help you along the path.

Find A Spiritually Mature Person

Find someone who is spiritually mature and can speak honestly into your life. Your pastor is there to help you traverse the terrain that you might be facing. Do not go to your most loyal friend who will tell you whatever you want to hear. They may be fearful of losing your friendship and then refrain from being honest. Locate someone who can help you by telling the truth.

My wife had to drive for several weeks. An honest, godly spouse is a reliable source of sound counsel. Allow them the liberty to speak openly to you. Do not be offended if they say things that challenge you. To be understanding does not mean that someone tells you what you want to hear; rather, they tell you what you need to hear.

If a doctor identifies an issue in your body, he will not promote healing by hiding it from you and refusing to discuss it. Ignoring it will not foster health. He must bring it to light so that decisions can be made concerning how to proceed. If surgery is needed, he will have to make an incision to reveal the issue. Only then can he remove or repair the problem. Likewise, we must be willing for our issue to be exposed so that it can be removed and healed. Hiding it will not heal it. Getting it into the open is what allows it to be healed.

Don't Stuff It—Address It

Some people were taught when they were young to stuff their pain and hurt. If something happened that caused them to cry, they were told to dry up their tears. Unknowingly, some were taught to stuff their emotions. The unfortunate result is that once these children grow up, they still stuff their emotions and live in a place of denial. They ignore their emotional wounds while thinking it is the path to healing.

The truth is that failure to identify and address these things will cause future emotional reactions. It is like the pressure of a volcano that eventually explodes. When the trigger is pulled, there will be molten lava that will flow on everyone who is near, and even those who may be dear. Stuffing things is not the solution. Extending forgiveness and receiving your healing is the road to restoration.

When my eye was injured, I sought help. We encountered something that neither my wife nor I could fix. We needed someone to identify and address the problem causing the pain. Failure to discover the issue would result in failure to get rid of the hurt. Thankfully, we had relationships that afforded us the help we needed. Isn't it interesting that what we needed was found in relationships we already possessed? Think about it!

The eye doctor identified my issue, performed a procedure to begin the healing process and eliminate the pain, and then prescribed things to prevent my cornea from being injured again. These are things that I could not do on my own. This is the reason we need the other members of the body of Christ. There are those who function like spiritual doctors within the church who help others identify their issues. They address the problem and the pain that is present. Then they prescribe a course of action to initiate and maintain healing.

Healing Is a Process—Extend Grace

Since emotional healing is a process, it is important to be patient and extend grace to yourself. You must realize that things will not change overnight. Rome was not built in a day, and the years of emotional baggage that you have carried are not going to be offloaded in the snap of your fingers. Allow time for this healing process to take place and mature fully.

We live in such an "add water and stir" culture. We expect results instantaneously. If we do not see things happen immediately, then we want to throw away what we have done and start a new course of action. Unfortunately, this causes many people to abort the process that was started. Understand that seeds do not sprout overnight, nor does a tree produce its fruit in one day. Healing will come, and the pain will leave if you stay the course of biblical principles.

When the "magic drops" were put in my eye, all the pain left immediately. However, total healing was a process that required me to depend on my wife. She helped administer the ointment to my eye and took care of me while I was partly incapacitated. She drove me to wherever I needed to go.

Although the pain of your emotional injury may subside quickly, healing is still a process. Until you can sincerely pray for God's richest blessings to be released upon the person who hurt you, healing has not been fully realized. You may not feel any more pain or anguish from the emotional trauma, but there is a progressive work that God does within you to totally heal your emotions.

Emotional Hurt Affects Every Area

The reason emotional healing is so important is because the hurts of the past are like poisonous gas that seeps into every area of one's life. The gas may be undetected, but it will slowly destroy an individual. The good news is that healing is available for everyone regardless of the degree of hurt. You do not have to live the rest of your life with the pain of the past; you can be healed.

When my wife and I traveled home from Orlando after my eye injury, there were times when I would stomp my feet on the floorboard because of the level of pain I was experiencing. This was so uncharacteristic of me. In past painful injuries or situations, I had always responded very cerebrally. Panic and emotional outbursts were not something I displayed. However, in this situation, the pain I felt had surpassed the threshold, where it breached my cerebral control and flooded my emotions.

This is one of the reasons that receiving emotional healing is so important. Failure to do so will cause one to live in an abnormal way. A hurt person will hurt others. They will react to things in a manner that is unbecoming and un-Christlike because they cling to the hurt and pain of yesterday. They will do things and then scratch their head in bewilderment as they ask themselves where that reaction originated. I can tell you the point of origin: It was born from the emotional pain and baggage they were carrying.

Anoint Your Eyes Daily

The eye doctor told me to put ointment on my eye daily, especially at bedtime, so my eyelid would not stick to my cornea and reopen the wound when I opened my eyes. This was key in fostering the healing process.

Likewise, I recommend that you anoint your eyes with the Word of God daily as a part of your healing process. When you wake up in the morning, bathe yourself with the water of the Word. Before you go to bed at night, apply the ointment of the Holy Spirit to the emotional wounds of your heart. God will heal and restore if you will just follow His prescription.

Healing is found in God's Word and the power of the Holy Spirit. Jesus is the only one who can heal the emotional wounds and hurts of mankind. He made you, and He knows how to heal you. Receive His healing and live free from the pain of yesterday's trauma. Let Jesus bring His full restoration into your life.

Paths to Healing

Here are some things to get on the path of healing.

1. Acknowledge the hurt or pain that is present. An ignored injury will not heal itself.
2. Find Scriptures that deal with the hurt you may be experiencing.
3. Speak aloud the promises of God covering what you are facing.
4. Receive healing in Jesus' name.
5. Confess and declare daily that Jesus is your healer—He is *Jehovah Rapha*.

9
DELIVERANCE AND FREEDOM

> Now when the Pharisees heard it they said, "This fellow does not cast out demons except by Beelzebub, the ruler of the demons." But Jesus knew their thoughts, and said to them: "Every kingdom divided against itself is brought to desolation, and every city or house divided against itself will not stand. If Satan casts out Satan, he is divided against himself. How then will his kingdom stand? And if I cast out demons by Beelzebub, by whom do your sons cast them out? Therefore they shall be your judges. But if I cast out demons by the Spirit of God, surely the kingdom of God has come upon you. Or how can one enter a strong man's house and plunder his goods, unless he first binds the strong man? And then he will plunder his house" (Matthew 12:24-29).

Deliverance is a ministry that is not spoken of much in the Church today. Unfortunately, it is very misunderstood. When you say the word "deliverance," many people envision something they have seen in a Hollywood movie like ***The***

Exorcist. They see heads spinning, bodies floating, and a minister holding a cross while sprinkling holy water. However, those things are not biblical deliverance. God never designed the process of being delivered from demonic oppression to resemble any horror movie that may have been produced.

Deliverance is not frightening or scary. It is something that should be welcomed and embraced by every believer. Not only should it be received with joy, but it should be coveted and desired. Christians should not want to be affected or controlled by demonic powers. We should all desire to be free from any influence of the devil. This means that deliverance is necessary for all of us.

There seem to be two extremes in the Church at large. There are those who totally reject the ministry of deliverance and casting out devils, citing that a person is fully delivered at the moment of salvation. Then there is another group that finds a devil under every rock, and anything negative that one does or experiences directly correlates with demonic influence. The truth is neither is correct; both are extremes. Remember: Error always lives right next door to truth, not a hundred miles away.

Deliverance Is a Part of Restoration

When someone is saved, their spirit is reborn. However, the demons oppressing them are not necessarily cast out at that moment. Salvation is the first step in deliverance. Your spirit is delivered from the powers of darkness, and you are translated into the kingdom of God. Yet, doors within our lives that have been opened for demonic influence will remain open until we deliberately remove the demons by the power of God and then shut the door.

Deliverance is a part of spiritual restoration. If the devil has control of any area of our lives, we are not restored. Jesus made a way for us to walk in total freedom and liberty, but we must receive it. It does not happen automatically solely because you love Jesus and have dedicated your life to Him. That is where it all starts, but it is not the finish line.

When demonic influence is present in someone's life, various negative issues will manifest. Loss of joy, sadness, depression, hatred, anger, and rage are just a few. Those who are plagued by these things will not understand fully why they are experiencing these issues. There will be no apparent reason for these fleshly displays, yet they feel that they cannot control what is happening. These are signs of demonic oppression that need to be addressed.

My Testimony

A little over 30 years ago, my wife, Stacey, and I had the privilege of being introduced to a couple that God used to minister freedom and deliverance to us. It was life-changing and eye-opening as we received from their ministry.

Both my wife and I were raised in a classical Pentecostal background. We thought the only people needing deliverance were the unsaved. At the time, we had been in the ministry for twelve years. We were traveling nationally and internationally, and God was doing remarkable things through our ministry. However, there were issues we both faced that seemed could not be overcome.

We understood the importance of renewing our minds, so we studied the Word, preached the Word, and prophesied the

Word. We averaged being in five or more church services every week. We were doing everything we knew we needed to do but were still encountering problems.

These things affected our marriage and family. It caused our perspectives to be skewed in about every area of our life. We would control and manipulate one another unknowingly. Our hearts were not evil, but there were behavioral patterns that were being influenced by something other than the Lord. We had unknown demonic oppression because of spiritual doors that were opened at some point in our lives.

I Received Deliverance

Once these things were identified, this wonderful couple ministered deliverance to us. It was like going from darkness to light. Things lifted and changed almost immediately. I remember when my wife received deliverance from a major stronghold within her life. We both hugged each other and cried together. It was glorious. The thing that was negatively influencing us was removed, and it felt as though we could breathe again.

Demonic oppression is suffocating. It will restrict areas of your life from maturing and developing properly. It will seem as though someone is sitting on your chest, and you cannot get them off. My friend, freedom and deliverance are so much better.

When we received ministry, our heads did not spin around, nor did we regurgitate into a bucket. There were no demons speaking through us, threatening those who were ministering deliverance to us. Neither did we levitate and float in the air. It was calm and non-remarkable based on natural observation. However, we knew that things had dramatically changed in our lives. There was a difference that we both sensed.

Demonic Influence Causes Defeat

Many Christians fail to walk in victory because of demonic oppression and influence. They try to crucify their flesh, but they still do not have the power to overcome. They recognize they are falling short but do not know how to triumph. Instead, they become controlled by forces that they do not fully understand or comprehend. They live their lives in defeat because they are unknowingly influenced negatively by demonic powers.

After their failure, they either go into a stage of self-condemnation or spiritual justification while blaming someone or something else for their shortcomings. All these things are wrong; they are dead-end streets leading to nowhere.

The next week, they see the same pattern repeat itself. It is like an endless merry-go-round that they are powerless to escape. Until they receive deliverance from the power that is enforcing this within their lives, they will continue in the endless repeating pattern.

Most negative patterns within believers' lives are caused by demonic influence. It is not because people do not know better. They do these things because they are unknowingly under the control of demonic forces. They may be good people who love God, but their failure to receive deliverance causes these undesirable repeating patterns to have power in their lives.

Deliverance Is the Manifestation of the Kingdom

The good news is that no one must live in that manner. You can live free, and you can be delivered. God desires to restore your life to be better than it was before. Deliverance is a key element to seeing this happen within your life.

Jesus said the manifestation of the kingdom of God was connected to deliverance. When the Pharisees accused Him of casting out demons by Beelzebub, Jesus told them they were mistaken and that the kingdom of God had come upon them. Jesus cast out demons throughout His ministry on numerous occasions. It was a common occurrence.

Think about this: If demons are controlling someone, God is not in control of their life. Technically, He is not King if He is not the one who is ruling. So, the kingdom, Jesus being King, cannot take place as long as there is demonic influence exerting control in someone's life. This is the reason that Jesus equated casting out devils to the kingdom of God being in manifestation.

If there are areas of our life where the devil has control, there is a hindrance to God ruling there. Those areas must be swept clean and then kept clean. The demons must be forced out by the authority of God, and then they must be kept out by closing any open door that may have been allowing access. These doors close easily once you are free of demonic oppression. The devil cannot reenter because he has no authority to do so.

The truth is that once someone is delivered, they find it easy to overcome the enemy. Most believers walk in holiness and act right once the demonic power that was being exerted in their lives is removed. Once that power is broken, freedom comes with newfound spiritual strength.

Deliverance Does Not Mean Someone Is Evil

It is important to understand that the need for deliverance does not mean someone is an evil, maniacal individual. It does not mean that they are spiritually flawed and deficient in their love for Jesus. It simply means there is something that is affecting their life negatively that needs removing. It means that God has something greater than what they are experiencing presently.

We must remove the thinking that the need for deliverance reflects weakness and spiritual deficiency. We would never think this of someone who had a tumor that needed to be removed from their body, nor would we think this of someone who had a tooth that needed to be extracted. Truthfully, we would encourage them to go to a medical professional to get the help they need to alleviate the issue. They would be commended for doing so.

However, in the Church, our view of people needing deliverance has been less than stellar. They have been seen as demonized individuals and sometimes ridiculed by church members. They are like the lepers we read about in the Bible. This only adds insult to injury. It is difficult enough that they are oppressed in an area of their life, but then being kicked for it makes things worse. This must change in the Church.

Every believer needs to experience deliverance ministry. I told our church body for years, "*You are either in a church that casts out devils, or you are in one that is full of them.*" Unfortunately, many churches have chosen the latter. As a result, demonic activity is allowed to manifest throughout the church.

Discerning of Spirits

Many years ago, I had the privilege of leading worship on Integrity's Hosanna! Music® Praise and Worship recording, ***Victor's Crown***. At the live taping, I had the opportunity to meet one of the individuals who helped in the production of the album. As soon as I met him, the Holy Spirit revealed to me that he was engaged in sexual sin. This was something God revealed to me without me asking or praying; it just happened unexpectedly.

About a week after the recording, I called and talked with one of the executives at Integrity Music®. I asked them if they knew much about this individual since he was working for them at the time. I was informed that he was professionally qualified and had been vetted thoroughly. I then told them what the Lord revealed to me. I also told them that I hoped to be wrong, but I was confident that I heard from the Lord.

People Perish for Lack of Knowledge

Several weeks later, I received a call from the same executive to whom I had spoken. He shared with me that a meeting was held with the executives and production team the previous week. During the meeting, it was revealed in a very unusual manner that the man I spoke to them about was engaged in a sinful sexual lifestyle. He admitted to doing so and then repented before them.

He went on to tell them it had been going on for over two decades. He said he had gone to his pastor (of an evangelical church) and was told he would just have to live with it and learn to deal with it. This pastor did not believe in deliverance ministry, and to him, these things were merely personality traits. So, this bound individual lived oppressed for decades because there was no deliverance ministry available in his church. This is the reason I say that churches are either casting out devils or full of them. People perish for a lack of knowledge, as this gentleman was experiencing.

The good news is that the men who were leaders of Integrity Music® believed in deliverance ministry. They ministered to him and then got him some additional help for him. He did not even realize that help was available. It had always been said to be a personality issue to be wrestled with for the remainder of his life. Wow!

Thank God we know that deliverance is the children's bread. It belongs to every child of God. The things you are facing are not just personality traits that you will have to struggle with for the remainder of your life. You can live in freedom and victory. You can be totally restored and be better than before!

Demonic Influence Causes Sinful Lifestyles

When demonic spirits control people, they engage in sinful acts. Every time a person sins, it strengthens the hold of the enemy within their life. The more they engage in sinful activity, the stronger the bondage becomes. With every fleeting moment, satan is squeezing the life out of these individuals. It is like a snake coiled around its prey, constricting the very breath from their body.

Christians who are controlled by these spirits will, many times, feel conviction and then pray for forgiveness. Their intention was not to sin, but the compulsion was so strong that they had no power to keep from doing otherwise. Condemnation then ensues as they question how they could do the things they did. The entire time satan's strategy is playing out, which is to bring separation between God and man.

The Goal Is to Separate

This is the way and manner that demons work and operate. They are not so much interested in merely leveling some sort of pain or harm to mankind; the end goal is to sever and separate man from a loving Savior. This is the reason that deliverance is such an important ministry that needs to be active in the Church today.

Demonic influence and control in people's lives are linked to every problem that we face today. The devil seeks to wreak havoc and chaos in the lives of all to which he has access. He does not care if you are saved or unsaved. Truthfully, he prefers the saved because they become like a trophy of achievement for his dark kingdom. The unsaved are already on his shelf, but to control and manipulate someone who has turned their life over to Jesus is hell's objective and goal. That is the reason that the devil will battle for the minds and hearts of Christians.

Spiritual Warfare

We must understand that we are in a real ongoing spiritual warfare. The apostle Paul stated that we are not wrestling and warring with flesh and blood (people), but rather with demonic principalities and powers which seek to control. To combat the enemy, we must daily pick up our spiritual weapons and fight the good fight of faith. We do this with the Word of God, the power of the Holy Spirit, praise, worship, and prayer, to name a few.

As important as it is to love Jesus, we must equally fight and war against the devil. Many believers say they love the Lord, but the problem is that they still are having an affair with sin. The Bible declares that Jesus hated iniquity and loved righteousness. The same must be said about us. If we continue a love fest with sin, it will give demons a doorway of authority to control our lives. We must close the door and keep it shut through righteous living.

Through spiritual warfare, we can ward off every attack of hell. We are empowered to see victory manifest as we overcome the schemes of satan. We have been given power and authority over every demonic force of hell; we only need to use it. Any wicked spirit that would attempt to thwart us will be crushed beneath our feet, and we will see total restoration in our lives!

Many Christians think that deliverance ministry is only for those who are unsaved and totally possessed by demons. However, deliverance is something for everyone, and everyone needs deliverance. I have never known anyone who did not need some measure of deliverance within their lives. Those who believe they do not need it at all are usually the ones who need it the most.

Possession, Obsession, Oppression

There are three distinct aspects of demonic influence that I will take time to mention briefly. Demonic possession, obsession, and oppression. **Possession** is when one has demons living in and controlling their spirit. I do not believe that the devil can possess a Christian. They are born again, and their spirit is one with the Spirit of the Lord.

Obsession is when demonic spirits control someone's mind and thinking patterns. This causes them to act erratic or impulsive. I am speaking of behavior that is beyond being emotionally controlled. It is as if they have little to no control over their thinking and conduct. Both unbelievers and believers can be obsessed by the devil.

Oppression is when someone is being controlled or influenced by demons externally. It can also be someone who has unexplainable physical health issues. This encompasses people who do not necessarily sense a compulsion to commit sin or evil yet still have great difficulty overcoming them in certain areas of their lives.

Anywhere Is Too Close!

Here is the understanding that we must all possess. If demons are affecting us in any manner, they are too close! It does not matter where they are located or whether it is possession, obsession, or oppression. The bottom line is that when there is influence or control within our lives other than the voice of the Holy Spirit, it must be eradicated; it must exit our lives!

Some people want to spend time arguing over where demons are located, whether they are in, on, or around someone. My conviction has always been that if someone is being influenced in any way, then they are too close, and deliverance is needed.

We should not be like the disciples of Jesus who desired to debate what caused a man to be born blind. These kinds of things are never fruitful. Instead, we should do what Jesus did and allow healing, deliverance, and restoration to be manifested.

You can debate over where demons are located, or you can receive your freedom. Arguing and debating will lead to nowhere. Receiving deliverance will lead to restoration. Which one do you desire?

Sin Is the Doorway

The primary doorway that demons enter is sinful behavior. This becomes the pathway whereby satan's influence receives access. Sin gives the devil authority to regain control of someone's life. This is the reason that we must make sure that we maintain a holy lifestyle so that we can sustain freedom from demonic spirits. You cannot consistently sin and expect to remain unencumbered by demons. The exact opposite is true.

Let us observe what Jesus said about demons and deliverance:

> "When an unclean spirit goes out of a man, he goes through dry places, seeking rest, and finds none. Then he says, 'I will return to my house from which I came.' And when he comes, he finds it empty, swept, and put in order. Then he goes and takes with him seven other spirits more wicked than himself, and they enter and dwell there; and the last state of that man is worse than the first. So shall it also be with this wicked generation" (Matthew 12:43-45).

Once someone receives deliverance, they must keep their house clean. Jesus said that once someone is delivered of demonic influence, the devil will attempt to come back and inhabit the place from where it was evicted. It is our responsibility to keep the door closed so it cannot reenter. If you shut demons out, they will not be able to host a party at your house. Satan will be forced to go somewhere else.

Why Is It Important?

You may ask the question, "*Why is it so important to receive deliverance?*" The answer is simple: You cannot experience full restoration in your life if there is demonic influence. There are numerous issues that happen when someone is under any measure of demonic control. These are also indicators that demons are present and wreaking havoc in a person's life. Here is a brief list of common things:

- Incapacity for Normal Living
- Extreme Bondage to Sin
- Deception About Normal Personality
- Abnormal Emotions and Outbursts
- Breakdowns in Marriage and Family
- Accident Proneness and Tragedies
- Consistent Financial Insufficiency
- Inner Anguish and Mental Torment
- Abnormal Sex Life or Attraction
- Gender Confusion

This is just a shortlist of things that typically indicate demonic influence within someone's life. These things do not make them evil or wicked. It means that they need deliverance and help. We must rid ourselves of the idea that individuals struggling in areas of their lives make them bad people.

We are called to be light in the darkness and hope to the hopeless. We have been anointed to both minister and receive deliverance. Let us allow compassion to arise for those who are bound and need freedom. The truth is that Jesus is the only one who has the power to set people free. He is willing to deliver all who call upon His name.

Misconceptions That Prevent Deliverance

Many people have misconceptions that produce fear in their lives. Some think that if they receive deliverance, all their "stuff" is going to be broadcast. They are afraid of being exposed. That fear prevents them from receiving their freedom.

The truth is others already know what is taking place in your life. People manifest outwardly the demonic influence within their lives; it is usually evident. There is no reason to fear exposure; this is just a tool the enemy is using to prevent you from receiving what Jesus purchased for you. The devil is a liar. Do not allow fear to hold you back.

Another misconception many people have is that people will think less of them if they know the truth. This is called the fear of rejection. The truth is that people will have an elevated opinion of you once deliverance and freedom are realized in your life. How many times have we heard stories of people who overcame drug addictions and made a comeback? Most people praise them for their accomplishment. Truthfully, people love comeback stories. Your life can be one, too, if you allow Him to do it.

Fear of Addressing the Issue

Yet, another issue that keeps many from receiving their deliverance is the thought that if they hash up any of the old things, it will only make things worse. It is the concern that addressing the issue will cause it to become greater. This is usually connected to a fear of confrontation. The truth is that the more you attempt to avoid the things plaguing you, the worse they will become. The stronghold will only strengthen if it remains unaddressed. The sooner you allow those things to be confronted and removed from your life, the quicker you will see restoration.

The biggest lie that the enemy will use is that there is no need for you to receive deliverance. Unfortunately, those who reject deliverance will needlessly live tormented for their entire existence. They will not seek help because they live in a state of denial. The fear of the truth prevents them from receiving their freedom and liberty.

The way to overcome the lie of the enemy is through honesty and transparency before God. Allow the Holy Spirit to reveal any hidden or secret thing that He desires to heal and make new. He will be faithful to reveal it if you will only ask Him. The key is to admit that the issue exists and ask the Lord to deliver you. He cannot remove anything from you that you deny is present. We must confess our sins, and then He will be faithful to forgive and deliver us.

Receive Your Deliverance

God desires to restore those who are bound. He wants to liberate those who are controlled by demonic influence. You just have to receive what He has already made available for you. If you ask Him, He will be faithful to do it for you!

Healing and deliverance are the children's bread. As a child of God, you do not need to live another day under the influence of the devil. You can walk free and enjoy total liberty. As you receive it, you will be restored. You will live better than you ever have before!

Steps to Deliverance

Here are some steps to receiving deliverance in your life.

1. Write down any area where you struggle to walk in victory.

2. Ask God to reveal any place where doors have been open for demonic access—then close those doors by faith.

3. Renounce all demonic workings within your life—tell the devil he has no right to you.

4. Tell every demonic influence to leave your personage—spirit, soul, and body. Cast them out, off, and away from you! Exercise your authority in Jesus' name.

5. Praise God and thank Him for your deliverance.

10

Working Together for Good

> And we know that all things work together for good to those who love God, to those who are the called according to His purpose. For whom He foreknew, He also predestined to be conformed to the image of His Son, that He might be the firstborn among many brethren. Moreover whom He predestined, these He also called; whom He called, these He also justified; and whom He justified, these He also glorified (Romans 8:28-30).

The above verses of Scripture are familiar to most believers today, particularly the one stating that God works all things together for good. Many have interpreted this verse to mean that everything that happens in your life, regardless of what it is, God is using it for good. Some even believe and say that God has divinely orchestrated these things so that He can produce His will and purpose within your life.

While I believe that God can take everything that happens, regardless of what it is, and turn it into something good, I do not believe that He orchestrates and wills for everything to happen. God can reverse what the enemy meant for your demise, but that does not mean He ordained it. He is the Restorer, not the Destroyer!

Apply God's Word and Principles

An actual contextual study of these Scriptures reveals that God will take all the things He is doing by the work of the Holy Spirit and cause them to produce a good outcome in our lives. The truth of the Word of God and the power of the Holy Spirit, combined with daily application, will cause great fruitfulness. This is the way that all things work together for our good. When we apply the truths of God's Word to our lives, then there is good fruit that remains.

Likewise, it is the application of **all** the biblical principles illuminated in this book that will work together for your good. When they are **all** applied within your life, not just one or two, you will experience the blessing of the Lord in a way you never have previously. You will enter true spiritual freedom that God intended all along for you to walk in. You do not have to live in bondage any longer. You can experience liberty and become all God has called you to be!

Forgiveness

Forgiveness is where it all starts. It is like a key that unlocks the door and causes freedom to be accessed. However, unforgiveness will become a spiritual prison that keeps you incarcerated and bound to the pain of yesterday. It will torment you every day of your existence. Unforgiveness is like drinking poison while expecting someone else to die. Unfortunately, you are the only one who is buried while your offenders casually pass by. It is just not worth it.

So many people, even Christians, hang on to their past hurts and pains. They rehearse daily the wrong they underwent through the hands of another individual. They eventually become bitter as they are consumed by the feelings they harbor toward another person. Unforgiveness is a hamster's wheel that can only be exited through the act of releasing someone else from the responsibility of the pain they caused you.

Jesus commanded us to forgive. He went on to say that if we did not forgive, we would forfeit our own forgiveness. The truth is that we all need to be forgiven, so we must all choose to forgive. It is not based on feelings and emotions; rather, it is a decision of heart. We forgive each other by faith! Remember, forgiveness is not for the benefit of the person being forgiven, but rather for the person who has been wronged.

Choosing to forgive will liberate you from the prison that hell fashioned for you. Forgiveness causes you to be released from the bondage of yesterday's experience. It is the first step to being restored and made whole. It will transform your life and make you better than you were before.

Victimization

Many people live their entire existence as victims of others. They live believing that the world is against them, and they are doomed in some way to a life of misery. This kind of thinking causes them to perceive everyone as a potential villain. Anyone could harm them at any moment.

Unfortunately, living with this frame of mind will only cause one to put oneself on the outside looking in. They will live defeated and downtrodden because they fail to see that they have been created to live as victors. The tragedy is that those living in this manner will view others through the lens of their victimization. This will, in turn, cause them to reject the very ones that can help them the most.

You cannot live as an overcomer if you see yourself through the tinted glasses of a victim. To be restored fully, you must rid yourself of this perspective and persona. It does not belong to you, nor should you continue to embrace it.

God did not make you a victim; the devil did. The truth is you are more than a conqueror, and this is the identity that you have been given. Assume this persona and give the victim mentality back to hell where it came from! As you do this, you will begin to see God's hand of restoration move within your life.

Family DNA

We are all born into a world of sin. Our ancestors sinned and opened doors for the enemy to afflict us with a variety of curses. Jesus came to redeem us from the curse, and now we are liberated by the blood of Jesus. The tendencies that came into our lives through the sinful conduct of our previous family members have no legal power to hold us any longer. We can walk in total freedom and liberty because the Son has set us free.

God visits the sins of the fathers to the third and fourth generations, but He remembers His covenant to a thousand generations. This means the blessing is greater than the curse, so the devil has no right to you or your family. Every generational curse stops with you because of the blood of Jesus. The blood line is drawn, and the enemy cannot pass it!

The actions of previous generations do not lock you into a way of life. You can walk free and experience the life that Jesus has prepared for you. There is no need for you to be tormented any longer. Today is a new day, and since you are a new creation in Christ, all things have become new. The blood of Jesus breaks every chain, and you are free. Let His restorative power create a new way of living for you and your future generations.

New Identity Through Renewing the Mind

To fully become all that God has called us to be, we must renew our minds to what He says about us. Throughout God's Word, there are declarations and promises that affirm who we are in Christ. Once we are saved, this is to become our new identity. The old identity (old man) has passed away. We now possess a new identity that is secure in Christ Jesus and forever settled.

Many Christians, after they are saved, continue to live the same as they did before they were saved. Much of this is due to the old identity that they maintain. Failure to renew your mind to what God says about you will cause you to continue believing incorrect things about yourself. Our belief systems are changed as we allow God's Word to renew our minds. A metamorphosis begins within us as we allow His Word and the Holy Spirit to reveal who we are in Christ. We put off the old man and clothe ourselves with the new. We move from a place of poor thinking about ourselves into a dimension of God's thinking about who we are in Him.

This type of thinking and believing propels us into spiritual restoration. We move to a higher level that God has designed for us to live. We no longer see ourselves as grasshoppers to be stomped by giants, but rather as giant killers on a mission from heaven. Our perspective in life changes as our hearts and minds are renewed by the power of His Word.

Your Words Have Power

Solomon said that death and life are in the power of the tongue. In other words, the things you say have authority to steer your life. If we speak words of life, then we steer ourselves towards its manifestation. If we speak words of death and negativity, then we will plunge ourselves into an abyss of needless pain and suffering. The choice is ours.

God desires to restore us and cause things to be better than before. However, it cannot happen while we continue to speak words of cursing and negativity over ourselves and what pertains to us. We must speak words of life and blessing to see restoration manifested within our lives.

Ceasing to speak negative words about yourself is a key to seeing breakthrough and freedom. It is imperative to discard words that curse not only you, but others also. This kind of speech must be removed so that we can fully embrace the fullness of God within our lives.

Choose to speak things that build and bless. Choose to speak things that edify and exhort. This will pave the road to the destiny that God has prepared for you. Your life will be elevated, and you will experience life and blessing.

Emotional Healing

As we journey down the road of life, things happen that can hurt and wound us emotionally. Words are spoken, things are done, arrows are shot, and spears are thrown that inflict emotional pain. It happens to everyone at different moments in their lives. Some people will become hardened in their attempts to be protected from any future assault. However, this response will only reveal the hurt that is there and cause them to hurt others. It is like the adage, "Hurt people, hurt people."

It is imperative that we receive emotional healing in the same way that we receive any other healing. We receive it by faith as we allow the power of God to do its work within us. God sends His Word to heal and liberate you from all hurt. His Word will bring healing to your emotions.

Many times, when hurt and pain are present, we may need someone to assist us in the healing process. Most emotional healing is not instantaneous; it requires time. It may be quicker with some people but longer with others. We must give grace to ourselves and others when the healing process is taking place. God will be faithful to heal as we are faithful to obey His Word and allow others to help guide us.

God does not want us to live with hurt; He desires that we be healed. His plan is healing and restoration. He will heal your emotions and cause your life to be different. He wants to make things better than they were before.

Deliverance

Deliverance is available to everyone who desires it. It is also required for someone to be fully restored and experience God's best for their life. It is a ministry that is seldom spoken about in churches today, yet it was a large part of the ministry of Jesus. He brought restoration to many as He cast out the demons that oppressed them. Freedom was wrought as they embraced the delivering power of Jesus.

The need for deliverance does not indicate that someone is wicked or engaging in gross sin. It reveals they need help to obtain the freedom Jesus provided for them. The truth is that every individual needs to fully receive deliverance from any demonic influence that is affecting them in any manner. It does not matter how little or how much they are being influenced; deliverance is to be welcomed and embraced.

Deliverance is the children's bread. As a child of God, it is your right and inheritance. Jesus has delivered us already, but we must willingly embrace it. It will not happen automatically. We receive it by faith, just like everything else that we obtain from the Lord.

Conformed to His Image

Looking back at the opening Scripture reference at the beginning of this chapter, we observe that all things work together for a divine purpose: to be conformed to the image of Jesus. We will look like Jesus as we allow these principles to be activated within our lives. Applying God's Word in every arena will produce good and lasting fruit.

It is imperative to practice these biblical principles deliberately and purposefully. It is more than just a spiritual exercise that is to be done only one time. It is a daily discipline and routine that should be a part of our lives. We choose daily to forgive and renew our minds to the identity that God has bestowed upon us. We receive healing for our souls regularly and allow the Great Shepherd to restore us. We pray what Jesus taught us to pray daily: deliver us from evil.

Living restored is not a one-moment magic formula. It happens because we consistently practice the principles found in God's Word. We choose to apply every principle within our lives so that our lives begin to reflect the image of Jesus. This is the way that we walk in restoration and wholeness. There is no magic wand or mystical prayer that will cause it to happen. Rather, it is a lifestyle of consistent practice of biblical principles and obedience to His Word. This is the way we live the restored life that God desires for you and me.

Be Restored!

God wants you to be delivered and set free. There is no need to live another day bound by the unwanted snares of the devil. You can walk in freedom and liberty; you can be restored. This is God's plan for your life!

We serve a God who heals, delivers, and restores. He wants to manifest Himself as *Jehovah-SHALAM* in your life. He desires for you to experience heaven on Earth, not hell in your house. His plan is that you taste and see that the Lord is good, not swallow what satan has shoved down your throat. Our God is gracious and merciful, not cruel and judgmental. He is the God who restores!

Begin to apply all these principles that have been articulated in this book. It will make a dramatic difference within your life. You will experience life on a higher plane. It is a place that God has already prepared for you. Embrace it and receive it in Jesus' name!

About the Author

DR. ROBERT GAY is the founder of High Praise Worship Center International in Panama City, Florida, and provides apostolic oversight to numerous churches and associated ministers. His vision is three-fold: Equipping Believers, Building Families, and Furthering the Kingdom of God. Robert is recognized as a prophetic and apostolic voice bringing a message of biblical balance and order to the church today. For a complete bio go to highpraise.church

HIGH
PRAISE
PANAMA CITY
HIGHPRAISE.CHURCH
Pastors
JOSHUA &
MIRANDA
GAY
SCAN FOR
MORE INFO
HIGH
PRAISE
CRESTVIEW
HIGHPRAISECRESTVIEW.COM
Pastors
MICAH &
CHELSEA
GAY
SCAN FOR
MORE INFO

Silencing The Enemy With Praise
Pastor Robert Gay

Praise and worship are more than words and music says author Pastor Robert Gay. Praise is a weapon of warfare. God will fight for you as you praise the greatness of His name.

"The contents of this book can revolutionize your life...It brings new understanding about the power of praise and worship."
-Dr. Bill Hamon

Planted
Pastor Robert Gay

Robert Gay confronts common "church issues" head on. He teaches with clarity and compassion that God is the Master Gardener who lovengly tends to every individual planted in His garden. You will find out how God wants to plant you so that you will flourish and grow and become everything He wants you to be.

"Every Pastor will appreciate this book...every saint of God should read this book..." - Dr. Bill Hamon

Best Of Robert Gay
Pastor Robert Gay

This compilation album represents some of Robert's most impactful songs that have touched the body of Christ throughout the world. This cd is packed full with 19 tracks that include powerful songs such as Mighty Man of War, Lord Sabaoth, On Bended Knee, Holy is Your Name, One Voice, No Other Name and much more!

HIGH PRAISE MEDIA PRODUCTS for more products or to order any of these products visit our online store at
WWW.HIGHPRAISEPC.COM/ONLINE-STORE

Sonship
Pastor Joshua Gay

Discover the life of a true son through study of the Scripture and powerful testimonies. The author shines the light on many pitfalls that ensnare today's generation while revealing the true picture of faithful spiritual sons and daughters.

"This book needs to be read by every person who wants to be a true son or father according to God's order." - Dr. Bill Hamon

Faith Force Academy LIVE DVD
Volume 1: Meet The Faith Force

Join the Faith Force Heroes and Professors M & C in *Faith Force Academy LIVE!* as they teach you how to become strong superheroes of faith! This volume contains 4 exciting episodes that kids of all ages will be sure to enjoy. Each episode features exciting praise & worship, step by step teaching of scripture memory verses, incredible life-sized characters, & illustrated sermons.

Faith Force Academy LIVE DVD
Volume 2: Faith Is The Victory

Join the Faith Force Heroes and Professors M & C in *Faith Force Academy LIVE!* as they teach you how faith is our victory! This volume contains 4 exciting episodes that kids of all ages will be sure to enjoy. Each episode features exciting praise & worship, step by step teaching of scripture memory verses, incredible life-sized characters, & illustrated sermons.

Jesus In 3D
Pastor Robert Gay

Do you want to express the life of God in every aspect of your life? In your ministry? For us to walk in the totality of Jesus, we must first cherish the fullness of His ministry. Every dimension of the ministry of Jesus is critical for us to have ultimate effectiveness for the kingdom of God. Today, if you want to reflect the life of God, you must receive and activate all that He did, everything He said, and everything He demonstrated.

Revolutionaires
Pastor Joshua Gay

Revolutionaries declares to readers that God is raising up a transformation generation in the earth today. Discover the life of a spiritual revolutionary through the study of scripture and parallels from history.

"...if you read this book you are going to be enlightened, motivated and activated into being one of God's "Revolutionaries." - Dr. Bill Hamon

Building Strong
Pastor Robert Gay

There is a blueprint that the Father has rendered for the design of the Church. Jesus has been given the responsibility of building what was in the mind of the Father from creation. The Holy Spirit is the agent that empowers and gifts the spiritual subcontractors here on earth to build according to the plan that has been rendered from heaven.

HIGH PRAISE MEDIA PRODUCTS for more products or to order any of these products visit our online store at **WWW.HIGHPRAISEPC.COM/ONLINE-STORE**

iBelong clearly and concisely articulates the need for every Christian to belong to a body of believers. With both scriptural and practical principles, the reality that every Christian has a function and ministry is clearly revealed.
FINDING YOUR PLACE IN THE BODY OF CHRIST
iBELONG
ROBERT GAY
ORDER TODAY AT HIGHPRAISE.SHOP
OR CALL 850.874.9745

NOT
MY
FATHER

GET THE NEW WORSHIP ALBUM FROM
HIGH PRAISE WORSHIP
GOD
OF THE
TURNAROUND
HIGH PRAISE WORSHIP
ORDER CD COPY BY CALLING (850) 874-9745
OR STREAM AND DOWNLOAD FROM
YOUR FAVORITE MUSIC PLATFORM
Available on iTunes
Listen On Spotify
available on amazonmusic